THE FEARKILLER GENERATION

The Fear Killer Generation
© 2008 by Kevin Shrum and John Pisciotta

www.thefearkiller.com

Design by Doug Powell

Dedications

from John

to my wife Robin
you inspire me daily to
ask/do/attempt,
great things for a great God

from Kevin

to Janet, love of my life
to Sarah and Keith – new in marriage and ministry
to Caleb and Isaac, my young theologians

TABLE OF CONTENTS

The Call

The Challenge

ConfrontΛtion

TransformΛtion

Acknowledgements

Writing a book is like giving birth to a baby. John and I had no experience with either...until now (that is, we now have experience writing a book; the baby thing will leave to the ladies). It has been a labor of love. Putting an idea on paper is a challenging thing. As a music producer, John understood the process of connecting sound with words. As an essayist and article writer of some note, Kevin understood brevity within a confined number of words and space. But to take an idea and put it in book form was a challenge that neither of us anticipated.

Writing a book is never done in isolation. Although writing is an individual activity, good writing is done in community as well. This is why there are many people we would like to thank. Of course, both of us would like to thank our wives. Janet and Robin have been consistent in their belief in this project. Both have been encouraging, helpful and supportive. Without them this project would not have come to completion.

We would like to acknowledge the readers who helped with the editing of the manuscript and who gave insightful suggestions that made the contents of this book more accessible to the reader. Thanks must go to Janet Shrum, Kristie Wilson, Laura Erlanson Jenny Stika, David Huffman, and Doug and Kim Ryan. We also want to thank Doug Powell for formatting the text and for designing the book cover.

It would be a great oversight if we did not thank Kent Shingleton, Youth Ministry Specialist for the Tennessee Baptist Convention and a dear friend who has supported the writing of this book from the beginning. Kent provided the opportunity that led to the production of this book. We will forever be thankful for his friendship, trust, and support.

Finally, we are humbled by and thankful to our great God who has graced our lives with salvation and who, we believe, has given us an idea worth writing about – the fear killing power of Jesus Christ. Apart from Him there is no life. Without Him there is only fear. May His name be praised and may the fear-killing power of the gospel of Jesus Christ set a new generation free from the shackles of fear and intimidation.

Forward

Invincible?

Our culture has convinced teenagers to live for the moment. Advertisers scream empty hype hoping to gain the attention and money of this generation. Their claims seem so promising. Buy our product and life will be perfect! Teens are literally addicted to laptops, cell phones, media downloads, and social networking web sites. Life and relationships happen fast.

Many parents have become enablers allowing teens to live out the "it's all about me" lifestyle. Moms and dads make sacrifices so their teenager can have all the 'stuff'. I wonder if we will ever realize that most of the 'stuff' is empty, temporary, and meaningless?

Our public schools are under pressure. Cheating, disrespect, and arrogance flourish in middle schools and high schools. A new sexual revolution plays out as teenagers have been anesthetized by a daily feed of deception. Lies and empty promises leave many teenagers asking the hard questions.

Look deep into the eyes of a teenager. What do you see? This generation of teenagers may look o.k. on the outside, but what is on this inside? Truth from God's Word reveals that this generation of teenagers is not **invincible** but instead **vulnerable**. I am reminded of the words of Jesus in Matthew chapter 9. "When He saw the crowds, He felt compassion for them, because they were weary and worn out, like sheep without a shepherd."

Most teenagers will not admit their fear and vulnerability. Their pride and head strong spirit simply will not cave in. But just think about what God can do with a generation of students who surrender their fear to Him and for Him! As you read **The Fear Killer**, I believe that you are going to clearly see for the very first time the journey that Jesus Christ has designed for your life!

And by the way, many of those hard questions you have been asking are about to be answered as you read the pages of this God inspired book!

I can't wait to see what God does as you fearlessly follow and serve Him.

Kent Shingleton
Youth Evangelism Specialist and dad to three teenagers
Tennessee Baptist Convention

THE FEAR KILLER GENERATION

LAUNCHING A MOVEMENT

An Invitation to a Life of Bravery and Courage:
An Introduction to Becoming a Part of The Fear Killer Generation

Thanks for opening up this book. We're glad you have decided to check it out. Whatever you do, do not put it down. Do not set it aside. In choosing to read this book you are becoming a part of a movement we believe will sweep the nation. This book is an invitation to a life of bravery and courage.

For some, this book will be a challenge to read because it will require them to think. For you, it may be a challenge because it's an in-your-face type of book. So, turn off the ipod, quit text-messaging for a minute and read and think and live (John 10:10).

This book is filled with radical and dangerous ideas, radical and dangerous because it makes the unbelievable claim that God is ready to move again among His people, especially among students like you. As the prophet Joel wrote a millennium ago, it's time once again for young men and women to dream dreams and see visions of God's great purposes (Joel 2:28-32).

It's time for something new to happen in your world. We're not talking about new technology, new music, a new political movement, a new look or even a new set of beliefs. We're not arguing for a new theology, but a clarification of what we already know to be true, embraced with passion and excitement, seen in a new light, and lived out with great reward.

Technology will morph, music will evolve and change, new beliefs will come and go. Intellectual fads will sweep across various parts of the culture. What we're talking about is something new in people, a revolution of godly passion that will sweep across the nations. We're speaking of **The Fear Killer Generation**.

XII

It's a Movement, not a Moment

By deciding to pick up this book you have decided to become a part of The **Fear Killer Generation. The Fear Killer Generation** is a movement. In fact, a movement of people who have made a conscious decision to throw their fears to the wind and to pursue the dreams and purposes for which they were destined.

The term "movement" is used intentionally. Fads come and go, styles change, and cultural moods are constantly shifting. But a godly movement is when eternity invades time.

A movement lasts longer than a fad and has deeper and wider effects on people and the world in which they live. The movement we desire to see is one of fearless, faithful, Christ-centered living that has as its epicenter a radical commitment to Jesus Christ and His gospel, a gospel that eternally and temporally destroys fear.

It's Time

It's about time for this movement, don't you think? As C.S. Lewis described, too many of us are satisfied with making mud pies in a mud puddle when God is offering us a day at the beach enjoying the beauty and immensity of the ocean.

This book is a call for you to leave the ordinary and to live an extraordinary kind of life that glorifies God and rejects fear, anxiety, and worry. Why make mud pies when you can visit the beach?

The desire for this kind of movement is not new. Centuries ago the Psalmist wrote (89:6): **"Will you not revive us again, that your people may rejoice in you?"** We yearn for a generation of Joshuas who are called to live lives of fearlessness (Joshua 1:1-9) and who call others to do the same (Joshua 24:15).

You can use the term revolution, revival, renewal or paradigm shift. It all means the same thing. **The Fear Killer Generation** is a generation of young men and women completely surrendered to God's purposes in every sphere of life, church, science, education, music, business, the arts, and technology. **The Fear Killer Generation** embraces the command of 1 Corinthians 10:31: **"So, whether you eat or drink, or whatever you do, do all to the glory of God."**

This is not a cliché, and it's not over the top. It's a necessary revolution if the church is to be reconnected with the purposes and plans of God and if the gospel is to reach every dimension of life. The good news will be unleashed on the world in this generation by young men and women who are unafraid and brave in the face of incredible odds and systemic resistance.

This is not a cliché, and it's not over the top. It's a necessary revolution if the church is to be reconnected with the purposes and plans of God and if the gospel is to reach every dimension of life. The good news will be unleashed on the world in this generation by young men and women who are unafraid and brave in the face of incredible odds and systemic resistance.

God Moving Through You(th)!

Every time God gets ready to do something new He does so through stu-

dent generations and we believe He's ready to do it again. Just like God used a youthful Joseph to save a nation (Genesis 37-50) and a teenage King named David to rock a kingdom (1 Samuel 16), God is ready to use a generation of students to save the nations and rock the kingdoms of this world with the truth of the gospel of Jesus Christ.

More Than an Animal? Really!

Your generation has been attacked by a system of godlessness that has reduced humans to nothing more than higher order animals ruled by primal passions rather than noble pursuits.

Atheistic evolutionists argue that humans are nothing more than the right composite of cells bent on self-survival and guided by a self-serving morality called "survival of the fittest." There is no soul, no eternal morality, no spirituality, no permanent ethics. We're all simply doing the best we can, getting all that we can get before we become fodder for the worms.

Why should you be surprised when one of your friends acts like an animal – driven by pure hormones and physical appetites – when the establishment has been telling them that they are nothing more than a highly evolved animal trying to make themselves "fit enough" to survive?

Why should you be surprised when one of your friends acts like an animal – driven by pure hormones and physical appetites – when the establishment has been telling them that they are nothing more than a highly evolved animal trying to make themselves "fit enough" to survive?

But you know this not to be true because you feel eternity beating in your chest and rushing through you mind. You are more and you know it.

And What About the Atheists?

Strident atheists like Richard Dawkins (*The God Delusion*), Sam Harris (*Letter to a Christian Nation*), Daniel C. Dennett (*Breaking the Spell: Religion as a Natural Phenomenon*) and Christopher Hitchens (*God is Not Good*) have once again called into question the very idea of God and the worthy pursuits of life, striking fear in the hearts of millions and paralyzing many with inaction and laziness.

Their criticisms of God and their evaluation of people as nothing more than highly evolved animals have reduced many to cowards. Scripture describes such people as those who have "**no fear of God before their eyes**." (Romans 3:18) Though your atheistic and/or agnostic friends may sound 'intellectual,' they are fools for not recognizing the God of Creation (Romans 1:21).

It's Time!

It is time to take a stand against cowardice that breeds insulated and isolated Christianity. It is time to face, confront, and conquer the fears that stand between you and the higher calling to be a person of great faith who accomplishes great things for a great God. You can be a part of the fear killer generation by consciously and actively deciding to allow Jesus Christ – the fear killer – to dismantle and destroy your fears.

This call to confront and overcome fear and cowardice is based upon a single, but powerful conviction – Jesus Christ is Himself the fear killer. Killing fear does not happen through a program or a set of arbitrary principles, but rather through a person who surrendered His life so that yours' would not be squandered in sin, who atoned for your sin so that you would not be condemned by it, and who lives even now as the resurrected Lord of the universe, empowering every believer through the Spirit of God to live a brave and bold life for the glory of God.

It is time to take a stand against cowardice that breeds insulated and isolated Christianity. It is time to face, confront, and conquer the fears that stand between you and the higher calling to be a person of great faith who accomplishes great things for a great God. You can be a part of the fear killer generation by consciously and actively deciding to allow Jesus Christ – the fear killer – to dismantle and destroy your fears.

As you read this book you will be asked to acknowledge your fears. You will then be introduced to the Fear Killer – Jesus Christ, the Lord. He alone has the right and the power to destroy fear. The One who is to be feared is the only One who can kill fear.

No wonder the Bible notes that when Jesus was born the angels announced to the shepherds (Luke 2:10), **"Fear not, for behold, I bring you good news of a great joy that will be for all the people."** From the very beginning of His ministry Jesus smashed people's fears, dismantled their anxieties, and crushed their phobias.

As a result, the early disciples were unleashed on the world in a tidal wave of fearless activity that changed the landscape of history forever. We believe that God is ready to do this again – through you!

Who is The Fear Killer?

And what about The Fear Killer? Jesus caused as much fear as he cured – in a good way! Jesus, the fear killer, does not kill fear by completely eliminating our fears; instead, Jesus kills fear by repositioning our fears onto Him, calling us to transfer our fear, anxieties, and phobias to Him.

The Bible says as much in 1 Peter 5:7, **"casting all your anxieties on Him because He cares for you."** To fear Him, then, is the only fear worth having. In fact, to fear God is the beginning of all knowledge and wisdom (Psalm 110:10). And when you fear Him an awesome thing happens - your fears begin to dissolve. This book is about identifying your fears and how Jesus destroys those same fears. So, sit back and read with daring courage, taking a journey from the land of the fearful to a life of fearlessness.

We desire for you to overcome your fears and to live a life that has been set free from the bondage of anxiety and worry. Most of all, we pray that you will embrace the One who longs to embrace you in Jesus Christ. In the arms of the Fear Killer, we are fearless!

YOUR FAITH NEEDS TO BE GREATER THAN YOUR FEAR
- *JOHNNY CASH*

THE CALL!

Chapter 1

ARE YOU PART OF THE FEAR KILLER GENERATION?
what and who are we talking about?

A rising tide of bravery is coming, a wave of fearlessness that we want you to ride. It is a tide caused by a tsunami rather than a tidal wave. A tidal wave is a massive wave that stands up out of the water and that can be seen for miles, like the one in the movie, *The Perfect Storm*. You can see it coming before it arrives. It is expected. There's time to prepare.

On the other hand, a tsunami is caused by a deep oceanic seismic event – an under-water earthquake – producing a wave that roles along the bottom of the ocean and is not seen until the last moment as it crashes the beach. You cannot see it coming. It is unexpected. There is no time to prepare for its arrival.

The Young and Restless

The restlessness of your generation and the movement of the Spirit of God are acting like a spiritual seismic event whose epicenter is deep in the soul of the hungry and the passionate.

This spiritual tsunami is sweeping the country, making its way through coffee shops, music venues, church pews, high school cafeterias, church camps, and college campuses alike. Its tremors are being felt all over the place.

For example, no matter what you may have thought of the 2008 election results that placed Sen. Barack Obama in the White House, much of Obama's success was driven by newly registered voters, most of whom were students and young adults. Why?

Because, there was a desire to be a part of something new, something great, a movement. The promise of change and the excitement of being a part of a new movement – no matter how change was being defined - became the driving force behind Obama's winning campaign.

Similar shock waves are happening beneath the surface on a spiritual level. This kind of spiritual upheaval is unexpected because most expect your generation to be intellectually shallow and disinterested. It's still coming despite the low expectations that have been placed on students like you.

You know it's happening. You see it stirring in the frustrations of your friends. You hear it in their voices and see it in their attitudes. It's being talked about in private conversations, in small groups, and more and more, in public gatherings. You want things to change, to be less boring, and more exciting. You want God to build in you and through you a greatness that counts for His glory. It's time and you know it!

And it's coming from a generation that is eager to be set free from the shackles of fear and anxiety. Tired of cowardly living, students and young adults across America are emerging from the shadows of spiritual introversion to boldly stand for Jesus Christ, the authority of Scripture, and brave, life-changing living.

Tired of cowardly living, students and young adults across America are emerging from the shadows of spiritual introversion to boldly stand for Jesus Christ, the authority of Scripture, and brave, life-changing living.

Old Truth, New Form

The desire to reconnect with truth and the "old, old story" is taking new forms and structures. "Christianity Today" (CT, Jly. 08, p. 28) recently reported that "People young and old are flocking to hear – and be changed by – winsome arguments for the Christian faith."

In fact, during the summer of 2007, hundreds had to be turned away from a Focus on the Family-sponsored apologetics conference for teenagers. Young believers across the board are being emboldened to live with courage that is grounded in a Christian worldview and sound, biblical theology. The movement is happening.

The Wind is Blowing

But where is this renewed sense of fearlessness coming from? Of course, any God-glorifying, Christ-exalting movement begins with the Spirit of God. Jesus explained the work of the Spirit to Nicodemus in terms of an uncontrolled, unpredictable wind (John 3:8): "**The wind blows where it wishes, and you hear its sound, but you do not know where it comes from or where it goes. So it is with everyone who is born of the Spirit.**" The wind is blowing, sweeping across dry souls who yearn for spiritual storms to change things as they are. So, the Spirit is moving. Nothing happens apart from the Spirit of God. Nothing! So put your sail up and catch the wind. The revolution is happening!

Chapter in Review
Questions for Discussion

- How do you sense God moving in your own heart?

- In what ways do you see the Spirit of God moving in your friends, in your church, in your community and school?

- What would a movement of God look like in your school or church?

- How should you pray so that God's Spirit will move where you live?

- What would you like to see happen as a result of a new movement of God in your youth group, church and school?

- What actions could you take that would become the epicenter for a spiritual earthquake?

Chapter 2

"I'M DONE WITH PIZZA PARTIES"
(although I still love pizza)
WARNING: This chapter is hazardous to youth ministers and youth ministry

God uses "means" – stuff, happenings, events – to bring about change. Three issues are converging to cause this explosion of spiritual restlessness and confidence energized by the Spirit of God.

Pizza Party Youth Groups?
First, the movement is coming from a resistance to and a fatigue from the spiritually boring and trivial. Students like you are tired of the "pizza party youth group" where things are a "mile wide and an inch deep" and where people don't really care about people or the truth. There's a hunger and a yearning for something more, something deep, brooding, engaging, and powerful. The entertainment model of youth ministry doesn't cut it anymore (as if it ever did).

> **Students are tired of the 'pizza party youth group' where things are a 'mile wide and an inch deep.' There is a hunger and a yearning for something more, something deep, brooding, engaging, and powerful.**

You know what I'm talking about. It's where you come to church or attend your youth group meeting and talk about feelings to the exclusion of what God has to say. God cares about what you think so long as you care more about what He has said in His Word.

It's time to re-learn the truth behind that worn out, cheesy, but true phrase – "It's not about me; it's about Him."

There is no excuse or reason to be boring and uninteresting. Thank God for the technology that has made ministry easier. But how could God ever be boring? While the church is not called to be intentionally boring, neither is it called to "out entertain" the world in an effort to draw people to Christ. It's silly to think that the church can entertain better than the world. The church will never out "MTV an MTV generation."

Pepperoni Theology?

The "pepperoni theology" that is learned in the "pizza party youth group" cannot withstand the assault that will come from the challenges of life. College students quickly discover that the shallow, easy-believism of the pizza party youth group from spiritual candy-land doesn't work in a materialistic, pagan, anti-Christian intellectual context.

This is why the interest level in theology and apologetics is on the rise among college students. They're playing 'make up' for what they should have received in their youth group.

It's no wonder that in 2007 Holman Bible Publishers released the *The Apologetics Study Bible* to great fanfare. Students like you are growing weary of a pagan culture that is hell-bent on its own destruction and, at the same time, are rejecting a pop-style theology that is nothing more than a student version of a health, wealth, and prosperity gospel. You want truth and you want it straight up and unvarnished.

This is why, as a student, you must demand a Christ-centered, Word-based student ministry at your church. OK, let's play, eat pizza, and do crazy things. I'm game for that! But in the end, demand that Jesus Christ and His Word be front and center when it comes to the core of what you're doing as a ministry.

This is why, as a student, you must demand a Christ-centered, Word-based student ministry at your church. OK, let's play, eat pizza, and do crazy things. I'm game for that! But in the end, demand that Jesus Christ and His Word be front and center when it comes to the core of what you're doing as a ministry.

No More Paris Hiltons, Please

But trivial, pizza party spirituality is not the only seismic cause of the coming tsunami. **Second**, the renewed sense of boldness I'm talking about is also coming from a rejection of a pagan culture that is bent on the shallow, the silly, and the inconsequential.

It's still OK to be as current as ever on pop culture phenomenon. I still love SNL and all kinds of music, movies, and cultural icons. Who could resist Tina Fey playing Gov. Sarah Palin? Who doesn't want to know the latest 'top ten' whether it's music, books, TV shows or the hottest bands? But there's a growing sense that all the music, TV shows, and cultural icons lead to nowhere fast.

Artists come and go, music changes and evolves, clothing styles change and the "scene" is constantly shifting. The fear killer generation is looking for something more permanent, stable, deep, and grounded.

Artists come and go, music changes and evolves, clothing styles change and the "scene" is constantly shifting. The fear killer generation is looking for something more permanent, stable, deep, and grounded.

This is why when I walk into a Starbucks I'll often see a student reading one of Ayn Rand's philosophy books (*Atlas Shrugged*) or a John Piper (*Desiring God* or *Don't Waste Your Life*) book that he/she cannot understand but who knows it is important and who has been told that it's worth the read to discover truth and meaning.

For some, pop culture has simply become a hobby instead of a focus of everyday life. Too many Brittany Spears and Paris Hiltons have given many reason to think about the meaning and purpose of a culture that treats its young as products to be used only to be discarded like so much trash. In other words, some in the pop-culture generation are beginning to seek a depth to life – meaning and purpose beyond skin level.

And I'm Bored with God, Too – The Rejection of Status Quo Christianity!

But there is a *third* and even more powerful ingredient to this new sense of spiritual and seismic bravery. It is a dissatisfaction and disgust with "status quo, boring Christianity." Students like you are no less spiritual than previous generations. In fact, it may be fair to say that your generation is as spiritual as any generation in the history of the world.

I hate to say it, but the problem is not with God. It's with us – me and you – and the organized church. This is why many are not seeking spiritual expression through local, traditional houses of worship.

Fed up with denominational politics, committee structures, stuffy religiosity, and a church that has a limited concern for spiritual and social issues beyond the church building and more of a concern for maintaining the organization of the church, students and young adults are setting new trajectories of creative spiritual engagement.

Don't get me wrong. I love God and His church. But we have made God so boring, so mundane, and so predictable that people even in the church have misconceptions about who God is and what He is willing to do through and for His people. We've made God out to be a nice, cuddly teddy bear. We can squeeze Him tightly for comfort, but never fear or stand in awe of Him.

The rejection of "status quo Christianity" is giving new meaning to the term "loyalty", defining it around truth rather than institutional structures. Labels are out and authentic truth-telling is in. And much of this is coming from your generation that has become jaded by shallow church life, bankrupt doctrine, and rampant hypocrisy.

The Needless War is On!

As a result, needless battle-lines are being drawn between the generations as to what constitutes "church," a battle that is wrecking havoc in churches, especially in North America. One generation wants sugar-coated, soft, orderly, predictable, kind-hearted Christianity. The other generation wants God raw, powerful, straight-up, exciting, and unpredictable.

On the Way Home from Youth Camp a Strange Thing Happened

But it was inevitable. Think about what happens in your own church. You plan a trip to a camp with a great speaker and an incredible band, worship is intense and small group times break down walls and bring about spiritual renewal.

But then the whole thing "crashes and burns" on Friday when your youth group loads on a bus or a van to return home for what often feels like a trip back in time. Worship is mundane and not intense, the preaching is not immediate and passionate, and people seem to avoid intimacy with one another. Whatever gains were made on the trip are quickly swallowed up by a lack of passion.

But it's not all your church's fault. Many students tend to think that Christianity is nothing but raw emotion. So when the intensity of a week in the Word dies down, so does your commitment to Jesus and His truth.

So, what will it be? The decision is up to you. Will it be the spiritually shallow, the culturally trivial or the religiously boring? Will you fade into the next phase of life only to live a mundane life of your own? Or, will you sow seeds of bravery, courage, and boldness that will lead you to live a life that counts?

Chapter in Review
Questions for Discussion

- How would you characterize your youth group? Deep or shallow?

- What are the reasons for this characterization?

  » Lack of prayer?

  » Lack of Bible study?

  » Lack of paying attention to the serious?

- How much time do you spend keeping up with cultural events? This may be OK to a degree, but doesn't it all sound the same after awhile?

- Is church boring to you? If so, why? Is it the spiritual diet you're on? Or, is it you and your unwillingness to get serious about the things of God?

- How can you translate what God desires to do in you to the other members in your youth group?

Chapter 3

The unChristian and the Mannequin

unChristian?

In his book, *unchristian: What a New Generation Really Thinks About Christianity...and why it matters*,' David Kinnaman has documented the nature of the wholesale rejection of Christianity among your generation. Kinneman's analysis, even if it turns out to be only partially true, is frightening.

What Kinneman documents is that "candy-land youth groups" and "status quo Christianity" produce students who are leaving the church in great numbers and, unlike previous generations, are not returning to the church. They are bored with the way God is presented to them and lived out before them. You probably have some friends who fit in this category – they used to go to church, but something happened along the way and... (you fill in the blank).

What Kinneman documents is that "candy-land youth groups" and "status quo Christianity" produce students who are leaving the church in great numbers and, unlike previous generations, are not returning to the church. They are bored with the way God is presented to them and lived out before them.

What's Up With the Old People?

Let's talk about your parents. Your parents' generation (the old people in the church) was interested in receiving the traditions of their fathers and mothers, maintaining, building, and even expanding these traditions. For the most part, this worked well for society in general and churches in particular.

But it had one major downside – it produced a generation of believers who hadn't really thought through their own set of beliefs. When asked, "Why do you believe what you believe?" their answer many times was a simple – "Well, that's the way it is." Or "Just, because." Many began to be slowly lured away from the "**faith once for all delivered to the saints**" (Jude 3) to a more cultural, pop gospel that was often unbiblical and ineffective in an increasingly pagan culture.

The results have been devastating to the church. The acceptance of a shallow, uncritical gospel has gutted the best of our church traditions, making those

The acceptance of a shallow, uncritical gospel has gutted the best of our church traditions, making those same traditions look silly and inadequate to reach a generation of sinners jaded by the hardness of life. This is why thousands of high school students are permanently leaving the church once they enter college or the workforce.

same traditions look silly and inadequate to reach a generation of sinners jaded by the hardness of life. This is why thousands of high school students are permanently leaving the church once they enter college or the workforce.

What is encouraging, however, is that many high school and college students (maybe even you) are beginning not only to question the routine traditions of previous generations, but to ask deeper questions about life, Scripture, the church, and all sorts of issues that have been previously off the table.

For example, the pastor and/or youth pastor ill-prepared for a Q&A time with a group of students will be caught off guard unless ready for questions ranging from ethics, philosophy, politics, sex, drugs, marriage, authority, and tradition.

Students are questioning everything. And I do mean everything: "Why does my church belief "x" and not "y" doctrine?" "Why do we take up the offering on the third verse of the second hymn during worship?" "Who wrote the rules on church structure?" "Why does my church not reflect what I see in Scripture?" "If I've already lost my virginity, what's the big deal about waiting until I'm married to have sex?" "How do you know what's right and what's wrong?" And so the questions go.

Whatever comes out of this major generational transition, there is one thing for sure – shallow, pop, status quo Christianity won't get it! There are too many serious questions being asked. And there is too much at risk to settle for the mundane and the minimal. The fear killer generation is rejecting this kind of status quo religion.

Whatever comes out of this major generational transition, there is one thing for sure – shallow, pop, status quo Christianity won't get it! There are too many serious questions being asked. And there is too much at risk to settle for the mundane and the minimal. The fear killer generation is rejecting this kind of status quo religion.

Bocephus, the Mannequin

I was speaking to a gathering of students a couple of years ago about confronting this type of "status quo Christianity". I decided to preach from the text in 2 Timothy 3:5 concerning religious people who have **"the appearance of godliness, but deny(ing) its power. Avoid such people."** My point was simple. The ruse is up. The emperor has no clothes. You must avoid being an "empty suit."

That is, religiosity, "churchiness", and false spirituality must be avoided at all costs. It's fake and everyone knows it. God wants the real stuff in you, you need the real stuff in you, and the world needs the real stuff coming through you! But how do you make this point to a worship center packed with students?

I decided to borrow a mannequin from our local tuxedo shop to help me make my point. You should have seen their reaction when I began to explain why I

THE unCHRISTIAN AND THE MANNEQUIN

needed their mannequin. It was a mannequin about six feet tall all decked out in a very nice tuxedo. For some strange reason I gave this mannequin the name "Bocephus," stood him up on stage at the church, and covered him with a black drop cloth.

The place was packed and the intensity was powerful as hundreds of students wondered what was under the black cloth.

As I begin to unpack the ugliness of the hypocrisy of false spirituality I ripped the cover off "Bocephus" to reveal a very handsome mannequin all decked out in his tuxedo. The crowd applauded. I told the students that "Bocephus" had everything, he had it all – arms, legs, head, fingers, shoes, a perfect build, and tux – everything except the real thing – real life.

"Bocephus" was an "empty suit." He looked the part, but had no life.

This is what Paul was warning against when he instructed his young understudy Timothy to avoid people who had the appearance of being religious but do not know its real power.

Paul did not tell Timothy to appease "empty suits." In very clear terms he told Timothy to avoid people who claim to have spiritual power, but are really empty and powerless (1 Corinthians 5:9-13).

The point is clear. There are too many "empty suits" among us. Let me say that again. There are too many "empty suits" among us. Too many in the church have no spiritual power and no real life. Too many in your youth group are shallow. They might be concerned about many things, but not the right things. This is why many cower in fear when the real tests of life and faith come.

Needless to say, "Bocephus" became a smash hit. No one asked me for an autograph after the message, but they lined up to take a picture with an "empty suit." You can laugh, but don't miss the point. Just as nature abhors a vacuum, an empty heart will be filled with something if it's not filled with God. God grieves over the empty heart. This is why the wind of the Spirit is blowing again, bringing new life and power to eager hearts.

Chapter in Review
Questions for Discussion
- Is a spiritual tsunami brewing under the surface in your youth group? In your church? If so, what are its causes? If not, what can you do to shake things up in helping lead your youth group to a deeper commitment to Jesus Christ?
- What does it mean to say that the winds of the Spirit are blowing? See John 3! How does the Holy Spirit bring revival and renewal?
- What three issues are converging to create this spiritual event?
  1.

  2.

  3
- Is it possible that an army of "empty suits" has invaded your student ministry and your church?

Chapter 4

WHAT'S DRIVING THE
FEAR KILLER GENERATION?

trivial Christianity, trivial culture, trivial church

So what's motivating this new generation of fearless believers? Why are students like you expressing frustration with shallow spirituality and easy-believism? Let me answer these questions with a question.

How did the "Big 12" do it?

How did a group of twelve men (the disciples) along with an additional handful of women and men (Acts 1:15) rock their world and turn it upside down for Jesus Christ? When the early believers began to spread the gospel in the regions north of the Aegean Sea near the ancient city of Thessalonica, those who opposed the Christian message said about these Christians, "**These men who have turned the world upside down have come here also.**" (Acts 17:6)

How do you turn a world upside down with no political power and no marketing tools? And how will you turn your school, your home, your community upside down with no money and no real platform?

Remember, those early disciples had no budget, no building, no youth group, no marketing program, no FCA, no True Love Waits movement, and no denominational sponsorship. They had no technology, no screens and projectors, no ipods, no FaceBook, no MySpace, no text-messaging, no twitter, no laptops, no game systems, no "geek stuff." How did they do it?

> How do you turn a world upside down with no political power and no marketing tools? And how will you turn your school, your home, your community upside down with no money and no real platform?

Answer! They had a strong, relentless, brave faith in the gospel that built in them a boldness to serve Jesus Christ. It was a boldness produced by the Holy Spirit and a confidence that was fearless and daring. For example:

- Acts 4 tells us that Peter and John got in trouble for healing a man in the name of Jesus. The authorities scolded them for this miracle. Peter and

John didn't miss a beat. They listened to their threats and then preached the gospel to the authorities. And what was the response of the authorities? Acts 4:13 puts it best, "**Now when they saw the boldness of Peter and John, and perceived that they were uneducated, common men, they were astonished. And they recognized that they had been with Jesus.**"

- You would think such an incident would have poured cold water on their passion to preach. Wrong! Peter and John actually went back to the other believers and prayed for even more boldness and bravery. Acts 4:29 records their prayer, "**And now, Lord, look upon their threats and grant to your servants to continue to speak your word with all boldness.**" Did God answer their prayer? Acts 4:31 answers that question, "**And when they had prayed, the place in which they were gathered together was shaken, and they were all filled with the Holy Spirit and continued to speak the word of God with boldness.**"

- And was this prayer simply a nice little prayer? And was this prayer meeting the end of the story? Or, did it have long term effects? Read Acts 5. Peter, John and the other disciples continue to preach fearlessly. They were arrested (5:18), but God miraculously delivered them (5:19). And what did they do? They kept preaching.

- They were arrested again and brought before the authorities (5:26). They were charged not to preach, beaten for their actions (5:28, 40), and then released. Guess what? You guessed it. They kept preaching and living for Christ. Acts 5:41-42 describes the outcome, "**Then they left the presence of the council, rejoicing that they were counted worthy to suffer dishonor for the name. And every day, in the temple and from house to house, they did not cease teaching and preaching Jesus as the Christ.**" I still find this hard to believe, but it's true. These men and women actually praised God for their hardships. They didn't back down, back away or cower. They stood strong.

I doubt that any of us would be beaten today for a belief in Jesus Christ. At this time in America's history it is not illegal to preach the gospel (although that day may come, and soon).

Yet, too often it's easy to lose your nerve to live for Christ in the small things, in your relationships, and in your daily witness for Christ. The good news is that there is a stirring among many young believers to throw off the chains of fear and to live for Christ. What drove the early disciples must drive you as well.

29

White Hot Passion!

I believe these same things are driving the fear killer generation. While some of your friends may have wandered off from (Jude vs. 3) "**the faith once for all delivered to the saints,**" looking for a more generic belief system, many are combining a warm-hearted compassion for the world with a passion for God's Word, for sound biblical teaching, and for the things of God, many of which are theological in nature. I see more and more students reading Scripture, asking challenging questions, and seeking sound, biblical answers.

The "young, restless" and reformed-minded believers of your generation, as Collin Hansen has detailed in his book *Young, Restless, Reformed: A Journalist's Journey with the New Calvinists*, Crossway, 2008, are attending apologetics conferences, youth events, and are reading theology, coming away with a red-hot passion for Jesus Christ and biblical theology.

The questions being asked are not "How do I get a date in a Christian way?" Or, "How do I get more out of my life?" The questions being asked concern God's existence and sovereignty in the face of bad stuff, the truthfulness and reliability of Scripture, why there is so much suffering in the world (it is the question known as "theodicy" in theological terms or the question of evil), and how to answer the critics and the atheists.

The Gig is Up!

The three issues mentioned earlier – trivial Christianity (pizza party youth groups), trivial culture (shallow living), and trivial church life (boring spirituality) – are converging to create the opportunity for you to seek bold and brave new ways of engaging a lost culture with an ancient gospel. It is to you and to your fearless and emerging generation that we write.

Again, the call to change or die is to every high school and college student, to every youth minister and campus minister, and to every pastor – *the Gig is up. We can no longer hide behind our religious walls, where unengaged minds have been watered down with shallow teaching and disinterested passion.*

It's time for you to shake off cowardice and fear and embrace the boldness and bravery that is possible in Jesus Christ. It's time to embrace the clearly articulated gospel of Jesus Christ. It's time to live without fear!

The Price Will Be High, but Worth It!

This emerging fearlessness will come at a great price – a Jim Elliot (we'll talk more about him later) type of price that you as a student, student leader, and as a student ministry must be willing to pay to see the things of God come to pass.

The trivial Christianity, trivial culture, and trivial church life that has invaded the Christian community has simply become the pressure cooker in which you must work out your own fears and anxieties.

The price you must pay is in facing your fears, allowing God to conquer them through Jesus Christ, and then fully surrendering all that you are for all that He is. You must remember the faith of past generations (2 Timothy 1:3-5) and learn how to stir up your God-given giftedness in the here and now (2 Timothy 1:6). When this happens, you will be able to live a fearless and bold life (2 Timothy 1:7).

Fainting Under our Fears?

And what are these anxieties? The conflicts aren't just at church. They're coming from every area of life. Families are broken, leading to insecurity and un-

30

certainty. High school is not as pleasant and exciting as it's made out to be in the popular "High School Musical" phenomenon; instead, schools seem more like war zones of competing cliques and petty jealousies.

Feelings of loss, isolation, and fear easily grip the soul. The Old Testament prophet Isaiah (40:30) was right when he wrote, "**Even youths shall faint and be weary, and young men shall fall exhausted.**"

Many youth are fainting and falling. Born of a "divorce culture" and disconnected from real and meaningful relationships (even though we claim to be the most connected generation ever), we have told ourselves that kids are resilient and that they will survive the selfish choices of their guardians. Yes, some will survive, but many will not.

Is There Good News? Yes! Go Green School!

But the news of the demise of your generation may be greatly exaggerated, however. A new wind is blowing. The spiritual winds of courage and confidence are blowing through a generation of students of all ages, backgrounds, and ethnic groups.

Fighting back the avalanche of fear-producing factors, students like you are braving the onslaught of a culture hell-bent on destruction with hope, courage, and confidence. Let me give you an example.

In the summer of 2008 I was involved in a student camp called Super Summer, sponsored by the Tennessee Baptist Convention and hosted on the campus of Austin Peay State University in Clarksville, Tennessee. This camp is unique in that those attending are divided up not by church groups but by school grade. In a sense, you are forced to meet people outside your youth group, outside your comfort zone.

It was my responsibility to teach students who would be going into their final year of high school. Once together, the "Green School" consisted of eighty-five students and leaders, filling the small ball room we had been assigned on the campus.

In total, 400 plus students of all ages and grades attended the camp – Red, Blue, Orange, Yellow, Green and Camouflage schools. Each night, all the schools would gather for worship and preaching. But during the day, the school that I led as "Dean" – the Green School – would meet for worship and the Word.

In addition to the four evening worship services with everyone, Green School met eleven times. So, from Monday through Friday, students were in the Word 15 times. It was intense.

And what did we study in those 11 times during the "Green school" sessions? We did not talk about how to have a better life, how to love your life, or how to hook up with the hottest girl or guy on campus in a Christian way.

We did not discuss how to catch a date in a Christian way. We didn't talk about having better self-esteem or overcoming "the blues". Nor did we talk about a number of the other trivial issues that so often plague preaching to youth and youth ministries.

For five days we lived in and dissected Ephesians 6:10-20, verse by verse, sometimes word by word and phrase by phrase, speaking of spiritual warfare and the armor of God.

We began by talking about truth (6:14a.) set against pluralism and relativism. We continued by speaking of the righteousness of God (6:14b.), using terms like sacrificial, vicarious, imputation, expiation, justification, regeneration, and sanctification.

These subjects were followed by messages on the gospel (6:15), faith (6:16), the nature of salvation (6:17), and the doctrine of Scripture (6:17). Added to these pieces of armor were prayer (6:18) and boldness (6:19-20). I preached about God's grace and power with as much passion and depth as possible. The results were amazing.

In fact, on Tuesday evening I preached a message from Romans 3:21-26 that I thought for sure would be over their heads. But I had already decided that if these students could memorize every word to every song on their ipod they could deal with some heavy-duty doctrine. I took the phrase from Ephesians 6:14 – "**the breastplate of righteousness**" and dove into the depths of God's righteousness and holiness.

And what was the response to this passionate, but doctrinal message? With Bibles open, the students were scribbling notes and listening with laser-like attention. It was stunning. Nothing replaces passionate, sound, biblical teaching/preaching. It wasn't trivial, cute, or shallow. We all almost drowned in the depth of God's Word.

But you could sense as we studied together that we would have rather drowned in the depths of God's Word than play in the shallows. There was a sense that we all wanted to spend a day at the beach, as C.S. Lewis wrote, basking in the glories of the immensity of the ocean rather than play in the mud puddles of life.

Catching the Wind

We mention all of this to say again that the new spiritual wind that God is blowing over His people is not some new fad or technique. Youth groups, college ministries, and churches have already tried to out-entertain the world. This is stupid. It doesn't work. The glitter is already off that fool's gold.

Besides, the way you reach people is the way you'll have to keep them, and sooner or later the next new shiny thing will come along and they'll be gone. It's not working. You know it, I know it and, painfully, the world can see right through it.

The spiritual wind that God is blowing over His people is the wind of spiritual power and confidence in the things of God. Your generation will be the generation God will use to change the world. It will be out of your generation of fearless and bold believers that God will raise up a new generation of missionaries like Jim Elliott, preachers like George Whitefield, and theologians like Jonathan Edwards.

Thousands of substantive, passionate students like you are pushing back the darkness that comes from fear, making progress by seeing and doing things on earth as they are in heaven (Matthew 6:10). Again, will you choose to be a part of this generation? He's calling. Are you listening?

Chapter in Review
Discussion Questions

- How did the early believers accomplish so much with so little?

- Is it possible to combine together white hot passion and emotion with deep and sound biblical teaching?

- Would you describe your youth ministry or youth group as shallow and un-engaged? Or, as unified, bold and confident?

- Read through the "Green School" event again. What does this mean for the urgency and expectation of your commitment?

- What is the Spirit of God leading you and your youth group to do?

AND NOW, YOU MUST GO AND DO THE GREAT THINGS
YOU WERE MADE TO DO!
- SHELLY

GOD, MAKE ME SO UNCOMFORTABLE THAT I WILL DO
THE VERY THING I FEAR.

WHAT WOULD YOU DO TODAY IF FEAR HAD NO SAY?

THE CHALLENGE!

Chapter 5

Boldness in a Bubble
fear is what is standing in your way

Cowardice exists because bravery does not. Bravery does not exist because fear exists. Fear exists where sin reigns. Sin reigns where faith is absent (Rom. 14:23) Fear is the absence of faith.

I have already alluded to it. There is only one thing that stands in the way of this rising tide of bravery, one thing that can cool the red-hot lava of bold faith and the white-hot passion of service – that one thing is fear!

Fear has a way of functioning like a bucket of cold water poured on warm-hearted love and compassion, cooling down its desires and passions. Fear has a way of keeping you from trying, from praying, and from risking the mediocre for something excellent. Fear has a way of paralyzing you. Let me explain by giving two examples.

Boldness in the Bubble

Fear can paralyze you when you make commitments to boldness in a bubble of spirituality. Let me explain. I like to jokingly (although it's really not a joke) say that I have attended hundreds of youth camps, retreats, revivals, and preaching conferences in my lifetime.

As the son of a pastor I have seen the good, the bad, and the ugly when it comes to conference music and preaching. I have heard the best of the best and I have heard preaching that would put God Himself to sleep.

I myself have preached many sermons for which, if I could, I would go back and apologize to those who had to endure my silly and shallow words. At the very least, most preaching to students and young adults underestimates their ability to grasp biblical truth and to grapple with very complex and important issues.

And what about the music? I have heard the melodious and the sublime no matter the genre; I have also heard the horrible and the horrendous. In fact, I've heard music that was so awful that I was embarrassed for both singer and listener.

Yet, while the preaching and the music are often uneven from event to event, one thing has been consistent throughout the many conferences, retreats, and revivals I have attended – unfulfilled commitments.

In the excitement of the moment, thousands of students have walked an aisle, raised a hand, and prayed a prayer only to walk away from that "commitment" once pressured by friends and life situations back home.

In the excitement of the moment, thousands of students have walked an aisle, raised a hand, and prayed a prayer only to walk away from that "commitment" once pressured by friends and life situations back home.

Unfulfilled Commitments

For example, how many students – and you may be one of them – have attended a youth camp and were stirred to go back and start a Bible study in their school or neighborhood only to see that commitment wilt under the heat of the reality of living in a pagan, Christ-rejecting community?

How many of your friends do you know who will have had a renewed love for God trampled by a secular hostility at school or in their community? How many resolutions have been made during a revival meeting or a conference event to live a holy life committed to Scriptural truth only to see those resolutions go unfulfilled?

How many students have made a commitment to stop engaging in illicit sex or participating in a pornographic life-style only to see that commitment fade under the pressures of uncontrolled desire?

How many youth groups (and even youth ministers) have been caught up in the emotion of the moment and made a commitment to become spiritual storm-troopers for Jesus, only to have the Darth Vader of home and school demolish the movement? And the list could go on!

And what lies behind these unfulfilled commitments and resolutions? I believe it is fear. It is fear that stops you from sharing your faith when you face the reality of unbelieving family members. It is a fear that comes from being isolated and alone in your school, where it seems that no one but you is interested in prayer, Bible study, holiness, and witnessing. It is a fear that causes you to back away from or drop out of what God desires to do in your life, your home, and your school.

It's one thing to be a passionate Christian with other believers – in the secure bubble of a retreat, conference or camp event – especially when there's great music, great preaching with great friends. It's another thing to be a passionate Christian when behind enemy lines.

It's one thing to be a passionate Christian with other believers – in the secure bubble of a retreat, conference or camp event – especially when there's great music, great preaching with great friends. It's another thing to be a passionate Christian when behind enemy lines. Unfulfilled commitments will result in a frustrated Christian life, and when you, as a Christian, become frustrated then you will become indifferent, apathetic, and cold. All of this is a product of fear.

A Gospel with Edges

But it's not just making commitments in the safe confines of a Christian bubble that trouble some. The problem with fear is that the very thing that could give you courage has been stripped of its power – the gospel of Jesus Christ (Galatians 1:6-9). That is, the edges have been taken out of what can be at times an offensive gospel. Why have we done this?

Sometimes, as Christians, we do this because we want to be accepted among our peers. We don't want to appear to be too narrow in our ways and/or narrow-minded in our thinking. All the uncomfortable edges have been taken out and smoothed over. But a gospel without edges is killing us!

We Have Gutted the Gospel!

The gospel has been gutted in two ways. **First**, it has been emptied of its meaning by including things that are not the gospel as if they are a part of the gospel. **Second**, it has been gutted by taking away things from the gospel as if they are not a part of the gospel. What do I mean by this?

The Add-On Gospel!

What I mean is very simple and understandable. Some preach what may be called an "add-on kind of gospel" these days. The core of the gospel has been added to with things such as how a person should dress, behave, where they should go and/or not go, and how they should worship based upon style and not content, making each of these things a part of the gospel (Galatians 1:6-9).

As a result, the gospel is reduced to a formula about how you dress, whether or not you should have a tattoo burned on your backside (warning – tattoos tend to sag as you age) or if you should have a body-piercing.

Such a gospel is external and does not get to the heart of the matter. It makes the gospel a matter of works-righteousness and not of God's grace and mercy in Jesus Christ. This is the gospel of psychological behaviorism rather than the gospel of the new birth that changes the sinner's heart (John 3).

To add-on to the gospel empties the gospel of its power. The gospel is not Jesus plus something. The gospel is that Jesus died for our sins, He was buried, and was raised from the dead victorious over sin, death, and hell (1 Corinthians 15). Salvation is by grace alone through faith alone in Christ alone.

38

Are Body Piercings OK?

The church I pastor is located across the street from a fast food restaurant. I often walk across the street for lunch. I've developed a conversational relationship with one of the young servers. I would love to see her come to know Jesus Christ. But to be honest with you, most believers in the average church would have big problems with her. Why? Because she has piercings all over her body, i.e. eyes, ears, nose, and tongue and who knows where else.

Do I tell her that she must remove all her rings before she can come to Christ? Or, does Christ take her as she is, where she is? If I tell her to remove her rings before she can come to Christ I have added to the gospel.

We must remember that the benefits of the gospel – a new attitude, a new sense of holiness, a desire to rightly live – are not the gospel itself.

Don't get me wrong – God cares how you dress, how you act, and where you go and with whom you go and what you do when you get there. But all of these things are not the gospel. How you act is a product of the gospel. What ends up happening is that so much emphasis is placed on doing, on dress, on styles, and other possible outcomes of the gospel that the gospel is stripped of its true meaning.

The Take-Away Gospel

On the other hand, the gospel is abandoned by taking out of it or not emphasizing the person of Jesus Christ, His atoning work, and His death, burial and resurrection. A "Christ-less" gospel avoids the real change God calls for through our sorrow over sin, repentance of sin, and in being completely sold out to Jesus Christ as Lord and Savior.

The take-away gospel is only half the gospel because it removes the necessity of sacrifice and personal repentance. It removes Him who is at the center of the gospel, reducing the gospel to a "feel good" story.

The gospel is that God was in Christ, reconciling sinners to Himself (2 Corinthians 5:16-21). The earliest expression of the gospel was recorded in 1 Corinthians 15 and it doesn't include one phrase about styles, behaviors, and attitudes. Again, God cares how you act and what you think. But prior to this you must get the gospel right or nothing else matters. A gospel-light or gospel-less Christianity is nothing more than legalism cloaked in "Christianese."

A Word of Warning!

If you are satisfied with an add-on or take-away gospel there is a scriptural warning you must hear. The great Apostle Paul started a church in the province of Asia Minor known as Galatia. He loved this people and preached the gospel to them, helping them establish a fellowship of believers who were bold for Christ.

But no sooner had he left them to start another church in another city, then they were preaching a different gospel, adding to the true gospel the message that all people must believe in Jesus Christ and be circumcised (which was an act of keeping the Old Testament law).

Paul's response to this add-on gospel that had also taken away the core of the message was swift and strong (Galatians 1:6-9): "**I am astonished that you are so quickly deserting Him who called you in the grace of Christ and are turning to a different gospel— not that there is another one, but there are some who trouble you and want to distort the gospel of Christ. But even if we or an angel from heaven should preach to you a gospel contrary to the one we preached to you, let him be accursed. As we have said before, so now I say again: If anyone is preaching to you a gospel contrary to the one you received, let him be accursed.**"

Robbed of God's Power

Gutting the gospel will rob you of the power of God. Taking the offensiveness out of the gospel is detrimental to the gospel itself. It sends a wrong message to those who need to hear and believe the gospel.

Let me be clear. I am not calling for you, as a Christian, to be intentionally offensive. In fact, you are to be loving, clear, concise, and truthful (1 Peter 3:14-17). While you should not water down the gospel, you must recognize that the gospel comes in "jars of clay" (i.e. imperfect people) so that God gets the glory and not you (2 Corinthians 4:7). This is why you are to give a clear presentation of the gospel of Jesus Christ with gentleness and respect. The offense in what you do as Christians must not lay in you but in the gospel itself.

Having said this, however, too many Christians invert this challenge and end up taking the offensiveness of the gospel out of the gospel. It is offensive to tell the sinner he/she is a sinner (Romans 3:23) under the wrath and judgment of God (Romans 1:18).

It is offensive to human pride to say that you cannot work enough for God to save yourself and that your works are sinful apart from being produced by the new birth (Ephesians 2:8-9). It is offensive to tell people that their sin nailed Jesus to the cross. It is offensive to rightly tell people that unless they repent and believe they will spend an eternity separated from God (in hell).

And there's plenty of Good News in the gospel as well. The same God who is holy and wrathful is also merciful, gracious, and loving. He alone took sin upon Himself and endured the wrath and judgment of God so that sinners might be saved. Through Jesus Christ, God offers the sinner forgiveness, freedom, healing, wholeness, and purpose. But you cannot take the edges off the gospel thinking that doing such a thing will advance the cause of the kingdom of God.

A Deflated, Powerless Christianity

Commitments made in the security of a Christian bubble and a gospel stripped of portions of its content will lead you to cower under the onslaught of the challenges of the world. When the gospel is rightly understood and fully embraced, it has the effect of empowering believers to be brave and fearless.

This means that the top priority of a powerful youth ministry is not having the best sound and lighting systems, the best music, and the most up-to-date technology. The priority of any ministry is getting the gospel right! When the gospel is right, power is unleashed, fear is overcome, and anxieties that have taken up residence in you are shut down.

Chapter in Review
Discussion Questions

• What is "boldness in a bubble?"

• Have you ever made a commitment in a bubble only to not follow through once out of the safe atmosphere of church, friends or other believers?

- What is the gospel? Take a look at 1 Corinthians 15 and make an attempt to outline the core of the gospel.

- What happens when I take out the important parts of the gospel?

- Would I describe my youth group as a gospel-based ministry?

- What could I do to help assure that we are centering our ministry around the good news of Jesus Christ?

Chapter 6

Becoming Radical and Radiant
two things fear killing calls for?

The Darkness Overcome

When I was a kid my family lived near Mammoth Cave National Park, one of the seven wonders of the world. Every time we had company I knew what we were going to do – visit the cave. In fact, the joke was that we had visited the cave so often that we could have given the tour ourselves.

One of my favorite parts of the tour was when the tour guide would explain how Native Americans and the early settlers would explore the pitch black cave. They would take an arrow, wrap the end of it in a cloth, and then dip the wrapped tip in kerosene, light it, and shoot the arrow into the darkness.

The arrow would land on a ledge or a cave shelf, lighting the entire room. Those early explorers would do this again and again. They would then make their way back through the cave until the light faded. It was kind of a "light, shoot and explore" technique.

They would actually do this "light and shoot" technique on the tour. I can remember the lights going out and not being able to see my hand in front of my face. The Ranger would light an arrow and shoot it up on a ledge, lighting the entire room. This always amazed me. A massive room in a massive cave filled with massive, blinding darkness and all of it was expelled and exposed by one single lighted arrow! Amazing!

The same is true of the radically committed radiant life. Don't say to yourself, "If I boldly live for Christ, the darkness in my school, among my friends, and in my home will overcome my small, insignificant light."

Light always expels the darkness, truth always wins out over the lie,

The same is true of the radically committed radiant life. Don't say to yourself, "If I boldly live for Christ, the darkness in my school, among my friends, and in my home will overcome my small, insignificant light." Light always expels the darkness, truth always wins out over the lie, and God's purposes will be accomplished. If this is true, then there is every reason for you to live a bold and fearless life.

42

and God's purposes will be accomplished. If this is true, then there is every reason for you to live a bold and fearless life. No wonder Paul would later remind his young student Timothy, "**God gave us a spirit not of fear, but of power and love and self-control**." (2 Timothy 1:7)

Radical

Becoming a part of the fear killer generation requires two essential things, both of which require the dismantling of fear and self-destructive anxiety. *First*, it requires a radical commitment to the fear killer Himself, Jesus Christ. You must become completely sold out. It must be radical and not just convenient. There is no other way. None! Nada! Zip! He is THE WAY, THE LIFE, THE TRUTH (Jn. 14:6)!

To embrace Him means to embrace everything about Him. This is what it means to be salt (Matthew 5:13) and light (Matthew 5:14) in a tasteless and dark world. Responding to the gospel of Jesus Christ because you have been drawn to God by His work in your life is absolutely essential. The Apostle Peter wrote of this kind of radical commitment and its consequences in 1 Peter 3:13-17:

"**Who is going to harm you if you are eager to do good? 14 But even if you should suffer for what is right, you are blessed. "Do not fear what they fear; do not be frightened." 15** *But in your hearts set apart Christ as Lord. Always be prepared to give an answer to everyone who asks you to give the reason for the hope that you have. But do this with gentleness and respect,* **16 keeping a clear conscience, so that those who speak maliciously against your good behavior in Christ may be ashamed of their slander."**

No Spiritual Frauds Allowed

The fear killer generation is not made up of spiritual frauds who are turning over some new spiritual and emotional leaf or adopting some silly self-help gospel. As a part of the fear killer generation you must fully embrace Jesus Christ as Lord and Savior as a response to God's irresistible work through the Holy Spirit.

You must overcome your willful resistance to God's grace and mercy as God grants repentance and forgiveness to you through Jesus Christ (2 Timothy 2:25-26). In other words, Jesus Christ is the epicenter for the tsunami that is coming, a tsunami that must begin in you.

A model for brave living can be found in the Apostle Paul who had his life revolutionized by Jesus Christ while on the road to Damascus (Acts 9) and who would then spend the rest of his life trying to get a grip on what had gripped his heart and soul.

The Apostle Paul would describe his spiritual progress in this way – "**Not that I have already obtained this or am already perfect, but I press on to make it my own, because Christ Jesus has made me His own.**" (Philippians 3:12) Read that again. Paul's entire existence was the act of making every attempt to get a grip on the "Who" that had already gripped him.

The Ecuadorian Five!

But Paul is not the only model of radical and radiant bravery. What about

the "Ecuador Five" as a model of radical Christ-centered, fearless commitment? The "Ecuador Five" was made up of five friends who were completely sold out to Jesus Christ – Jim Elliot, Ed McCully, Roger Youderian, Pete Fleming, and Nate Saint.

These five missionary friends felt compelled to reach an unreached people group known as the Huaorani Indians of Ecuador. They first made contact with the Huaorani Indians by using loud speakers from their airplane and by dropping baskets filled with gifts as they made repeated fly-bys over their village. They made contact with one of the natives that gave them hope of further contact, giving him the name "George" (real name Naenkiwi) and even giving him a ride in their small airplane on one occasion.

Plans were made for more extensive visits with more of the residents of this isolated and unreached people group. But January 6, 1956 arrived, a day that would live forever in the minds of many believers and certainly on the pages of history books. On that day, Elliot and his companions landed on a make-shift runway they had built on a wide place (what they called 'the beach') along the Curaray River near the village.

"George" had not told the truth to the other men in the tribe about his many friendly encounters with the missionaries. On the day the "Ecuador Five" landed, ten angry Huaorani tribesmen greeted the missionaries, killing Elliot and his four companions. Elliot's dead body, along with that of Youderian, Fleming and Saint were later found floating downstream. McCully's body was never recovered.

An entry in Elliot's journey dated October 28th, 1949, summarized his bold and faith-filled attitude about life – "*He is no fool who gives what he cannot keep to gain that which he cannot lose.*" That statement was written by Elliot at the age of 22 when he was a senior at Wheaton College. Did you get that? He was 22 when he wrote these words, not 42 or 52, but 22.

Wasted Life or Eternal Investment?

The question you have to answer if you are to live a bold and brave life is will you waste your life or will you eternally invest it for God? Some said that Elliot wasted his life. He was a sharp student, a brilliant linguist,

The question you have to answer if you are to live a bold and brave life is will you waste your life or will you eternally invest it for God?

and a fine communicator. Even some Christians said that he could have helped the kingdom of God more by playing it safe and becoming a translator of the Bible into other languages.

Yet, God used Elliot's bold and brave sacrifice as the seed that would eventually result in the evangelization of many of the Huaorani Indians, including Naenkiwi (George). Just six years after penning those profound words of commitment, Elliot would gain that which he could never lose – eternal life in Jesus Christ.

Hearing the Call

To embrace Jesus Christ - the fear killer - means to hear the call of God in the gospel of God, to repent of sin (and fear), and to turn in faith toward Him and, in doing so, having Him forgive every sin, crush every false fear, and dismantle every anxiety that seeks to strangle and stifle you.

In other words, to become a part of the fear killer generation is to make a radical, life changing commitment to the only person who can dismantle fear – Jesus Christ!

To embrace Jesus Christ - the fear killer - means to hear the call of God in the gospel of God, to repent of sin (and fear), and to turn in faith toward Him and, in doing so, having Him forgive every sin, crush every false fear, and dismantle every anxiety that seeks to strangle and stifle you.

This is why Jesus said in Matthew 10:28, "**And do not fear those who kill the body but cannot kill the soul. Rather fear Him (God) who can destroy both soul and body in hell.**" And who is it that can kill both body and soul in hell? The only One who has that kind of authority is God! Yet, when you fully surrender to Him He calms your fears, dismantles your anxieties, and resolves your worries. Will you be a part of this generation through whom God will change the world with the gospel of Jesus Christ?

Radiant!

Second, this kind of radical commitment immediately becomes radiant and bright! A radically committed, Christ-centered life is so unusual that it becomes obvious to all that something is different. This is what Jesus Christ does in the life of a once fearful sinner – the light goes on and something awesome happens. God bursts forth into every area of life. The sinner is brought out of darkness and into the light of the glorious gospel of Jesus Christ. Again, Paul would write these stunning words in 2 Corinthians 4:1-18:

> "**Therefore, having this ministry by the mercy of God, we do not lose heart. 2 But we have renounced disgraceful, underhanded ways. We refuse to practice cunning or to tamper with God's word, but by the open statement of the truth we would commend ourselves to everyone's conscience in the sight of God. 3 And even if our gospel is veiled, it is veiled only to those who are perishing. 4 In their case the god of this world has blinded the minds of the unbelievers, to keep them from seeing the light of the gospel of the glory of Christ, who is the image of God. 5 For what we proclaim is not ourselves, but Jesus Christ as Lord, with ourselves as your servants for Jesus' sake. 6 For God, who said, 'Let light shine out of darkness,' has shone in our hearts to give the light of the knowledge of the glory of God in the face of Jesus Christ. 7 But we have this treasure in jars of clay, to show that the surpassing power belongs to God and not to us. 8 We are afflicted in every way, but not crushed; perplexed, but not driven to despair; 9 persecuted, but not forsaken; struck down, but not destroyed; 10 always carrying in the body the death of Jesus, so that the life of Jesus may also be manifested in our bodies. 11 For we who live are always being given over to death for Jesus' sake, so that the life of Jesus also may be manifested**

45

in our mortal flesh. 12 So death is at work in us, but life in you. 13 Since we have the same spirit of faith according to what has been written, 'I believed, and so I spoke,' we also believe, and so we also speak, 14 knowing that he who raised the Lord Jesus will raise us also with Jesus and bring us with you into his presence. 15 For it is all for your sake, so that as grace extends to more and more people it may increase thanksgiving, to the glory of God. 16 So we do not lose heart. Though our outer self is wasting away, our inner self is being renewed day by day. 17 For this light momentary affliction is preparing for us an eternal weight of glory beyond all comparison, 18 as we look not to the things that are seen but to the things that are unseen. For the things that are seen are transient, but the things that are unseen are eternal."

Notice the progression of thought in this text. Paul had a ministry only by the grace and mercy of God (vs. 1). As a result, he renounced the things of this world and made a commitment to reject shallow "easy-believism" so that he might fully embrace the truth of the gospel of Jesus Christ (vs. 2).

He also knew that the "evil one" is real and blinds sinners to the truth of the gospel, so the stakes are high (vs. 3-4).

He must get it right so that the brightness of Christ in his life will be used by God to remove the blinders from the eyes of those who don't see it. This is why Paul is not all about himself (vs. 5), but is completely and radically sold out to the gospel of Jesus Christ. Jesus Christ is the light of his life.

Paul continues. The same Creator God who created light allowed the light of the gospel of Jesus Christ to burst forth in the heart of the sinner (vs. 6). This is why Paul said with confidence that though he may struggle at times, Jesus Christ was his life, a life that will rise above the "death scenes" of life (vs. 7-12). The security of this kind of bold living is the resurrection of Jesus Christ (vs. 13-15). Because the radiance of Jesus Christ had become his radiance, he did "not lose heart." (vs. 16)

When radical commitment to Jesus Christ becomes the radiance of your life then you can say with Paul (vs. 16-18), "***Though our outer nature is wasting away, our inner nature is being renewed day by day. For this slight and momentary affliction is preparing for us an eternal weight of glory beyond all comparison, as we look not to the things that are seen but to the things that are unseen. For the things that are seen are transient, but the things that are unseen are eternal.***"

46

Fear cannot exist for long in the life of a radically committed and radiantly gleaming life. Not possible! This doesn't mean times are always easy. It simply means that light always conquers darkness and boldness always overcomes fear.

Chapter in Review
Discussion Questions

- What are the two things required to become a part of the fear killer generation?

  1.

  2.

- How would you describe a "spiritual fraud?"

- Does the story of the "Ecuadorian Five" connect with you? How could such young men make such an astounding commitment so early in life? What did they know that many of us not know?

- How does Jesus Christ overcome the darkness in our lives so keeps us from a radical and radiant lifestyle?

Chapter 7

The Little Lady in the Big Dark Room
the threat in fear and the fear of threat

You might be saying at this point, "OK, I'm with you so far. Fear is a big deal and everyone has it. But you don't understand how afraid I am, how timid I am, and how intimidated I feel when it comes to this stuff. There's no way I can live a bold life for Christ."

To get at this fear thing you must understand what fear is and how it works. If fear is the criminal that steals your confidence, then what is it? How does it function? How and why does it destroy your courage, damage your purposes, and squelch your boldness?

Or you might be asking, "I know what fear does, but exactly what is fear?" *The Oxford American Writer's Thesaurus* uses numerous words that are interchangeable with fear: fright, alarm, panic, trepidation, dread, dismay, distress, the creeps, the willies, and the heebie-jeebies. But words don't explain the sense or feelings of fear that we experience when attempting to do something bold.

The Little Lady in the Big Dark Room!

Here's what you've got to understand. If you don't deal with your fears, your fears will deal with you. And when fear settles into your life, the relatives of fear will come for extended visits like anxiety, discouragement, self-doubt, lack of trust, loss of confidence, relational isolation, loss of creativity, and diminishing boldness. The consequences can be devastating.

I am reminded of the family that asked me to visit their mother in a local nursing home. I should have known that things were going to go bad when no one from the family was willing to accompany me on this visit.

When I arrived at the nursing home I found something rather shocking. In a room normally reserved for two was a single bed where a small, petite woman fully clothed lay with the covers pulled up to just underneath her chin.

The room was suffocatingly hot on a rather warm, summer day. The blinds were pulled and the curtains were drawn so that very little of the burning midday sun could break into the room. The room was dark in so many ways. I pulled a chair near the bed, took my seat, identified myself, and asked how she was doing. What happened next blew me away.

She began to ask me to check under the bed for demons, told me that the nursing home staff was "after her," that her family hated her, and that God had abandoned her. I tried as best as I could to comfort her, but to no avail. I prayed. I later learned that the reason she resided alone in a room normally reserved for two was that no one could get along with her. She had no physical maladies and no mental disease. The diagnosis? She had been lost to fear. How do I know this?

Because when I later asked the family about their mother they told me that her condition had actually started years before. She had been a generally fearful person. Small fears grew into large fears until she lost touch with reality.

She feared everything, then feared everyone and ultimately became so ruled by fear that she became dysfunctional and disconnected. And all of this started when she was a very young woman. I remember leaving the nursing home that day thinking to myself, "I do not want to live in fear."

But What Is It?

If fear is so pervasive, then what is it? How do you define something that seems to impact nearly every area of life, especially the most important areas of life? It's not enough to say that it's just raw emotion or pure feeling.

Fear does express itself in pure feeling and raw emotion. But fear is more than experiencing shortness of breath; it's more than sweaty palms and a palpitating heart. And it's not enough to look at the circumstances of life in order to identify what we're afraid of.

The circumstances of life can be frightening. But fear is something more than raw emotion that is caused by the circumstances of life. This kind of definition doesn't account for the absolute unexplainable dread you feel when it comes to various experiences.

Harold Clayton Urey (April 29, 1893 – January 5, 1981) was a brilliant physical chemist who served on the Uranium Committee of the Manhattan Project which developed the atom bomb for the United States. His main contribution was the development of the gaseous diffusion method that helped separate uranium-235 from uranium 238. He was awarded the Nobel Peace Prize in Chemistry in 1934 for this work on this process. What many do not know, however, is that he wrote a famous pamphlet entitled, 'I'm a Frightened Man' in response to the consequences of his own work that led to the creation of the one of the most destructive weapons ever created. He wrote, "I write to frighten you. I am a frightened man myself. All the scientists I know are frightened – frightened for their lives – and frightened for your life."

49

You may believe that fear is produced in you by a desire to avoid pain – humans generally don't like pain. The possibility of experiencing pain causes you to experience levels of fear that can be emotionally inhibiting and physically disabling. Pain is to be feared. Yet, pain can also be good. Pain warns you of coming danger.

The pain of a sore throat is a good warning sign that you are sick and need to see a doctor. So the experience of pain cuts both ways. We dread pain. Pain is never pleasant. Yet some pains are necessary, even beneficial.

If fear is defined as a reaction to the possibility of experiencing pain, then it reasons that if you are not experiencing pain you should not be experiencing any fear. But you know this is not true. You know it is not true because pain is something more than physical discomfort.

Fear is an emotional response to tangible and realistic dangers.
- Wikipedia

Most of the time you may refer to the "pains of life" not in terms of physical discomfort but in terms of emotional stress. So fear does include elements of pain, both physical and emotional, but is not limited to the fear of pain.

Joseph Stalin (December 18, 1878 – March 5, 1953), the maniacal ruler of the former Soviet Union, was such a fearful man that he lived with the constant fear of being poisoned or killed himself. He had eight bedrooms in the Presidential Palace which could be locked up like a bank safe. Nobody ever knew in which of these bedrooms he slept on any given night.

Fear is Something Deeper

Maybe there's something deeper and more sinister to fear than is first supposed. What is the very nature of fear itself that is common to all fears? Maybe the dread, anxiety, and the angst you feel are all a result of something deeper and more haunting than simply uncontrolled emotions or frightening circumstances.

It's rather easy to look at the circumstances of life and attempt to figure out what you're afraid of based on what is happening around you. You may fear getting up each morning and going to school, having to face people that may not like you or that you may not like. You may fear taking tests. But circumstances change, life moves, and emotions ebb and flow.

As a result, you will experience different circumstances, yet the same general feelings of fear, dread, and anxiety. There's something deeper, more frightening, more disabling to fear than simply circumstance and raw emotion.

A Simple Definition of Fear

Let's begin with a simple definition of fear. Fear is what you experience when you are confronted by **a threat to either your well-being or your being itself**. *In general, 1) fear as a threat to your well-being covers all the fears you experience in relation to your physical nature. 2) Fear as a threat to your being itself comes from a general threat to your identity as a person.*

Fear is a sense of impending

"It is not work that kills men; it is worry. Work is healthy; you can hardly put more upon a man than he can bear. Worry is rust upon the blade. It is not the revolution that destroys the machinery, but the friction. Fear secretes acids, but love and trust are sweet juices."
- Beecher

doom that will threaten you to the very core of your being. It is more than being afraid of heights or of water or of relationships. It is more than being fearful of the past or the future.

Fear is the product of having your well-being and your very being threatened to the point of extinction. It is the notion that what you face threatens to annihilate you or diminish your very existence. It is the sense of not only being threatened, but that what threatens you is out of your control.

"Fear is the product of having our well-being and our very being threatened to the point of extinction. It is the notion that what we face threatens to annihilate or diminish our very existence."

This is how the Apostle Paul described his own struggles and fears in the ministry. In 2 Corinthians 7:5 he wrote, **"For even when we came into Macedonia, our bodies had no rest, but we were afflicted at every turn – fighting without and fears within."** In other words, Paul experienced threats and accusations from outside of himself; and, at the same time, he experienced the internal anxieties of life within his own heart and mind.

Further, what may lie at the core of a fear of heights cannot be measured in feet and inches, but rather by the sense that you may lose your balance, fall, and hit the ground never to recover. In essence, your well-being is threatened. Water is harmless, but to the one who fears it, it becomes a blanket of death.

So, in brief, let's assume that fear is a deep-seated intellectual and emotional response to something that threatens your well-being and your being. Let's assume that it's more than raw emotion or frightening circumstances. And let's assume that the degree of fear you experience is related directly to the degree of the threat you experience – the greater the threat to your well-being and to your being the greater the sense of fear you will experience. So, what does this look like in reality?

- You may fear what other people think of you because it threatens your ego.
- You may fear sticking your neck out on a project at school because of the threat of failure.
- You may fear asking a particular girl or the guy out on a date because of the threat that they might say "NO!"
- You may fear being different because of the threat that comes with non-conformity.
- You may fear living for Christ because of the threat you sense from that which is anti-Christian.

Paranoia is a term used to describe a psychosis of fear, a heightened perception of being persecuted, false or otherwise. This degree of fear often causes one to change their normal behavior in radical ways, or even to become extremely compulsive. Sometimes, the result of extreme paranoia is a phobia.

51

Distrust in the context of interpersonal fear. It is sometimes explained as the inward feeling of caution, usually focused toward a person, representing an unwillingness to trust in someone else. Distrust is not a lack of faith or belief in someone, but a feeling of warning towards someone or something questionable or unknown. For example, one may "distrust" a stranger who acts in a way that is perceived as "odd." Likewise one may "distrust" the safety of a rusty old bridge across a 100-ft. drop.

Terror refers to a pronounced state of fear - when someone becomes overwhelmed with a sense of immediate danger. Also, it can be caused by the perception of a possible threat (possibly extreme) that would induce a phobia. As a consequence, terror overwhelms the person to the point that they would make irrational choices and engage in non-typical behavior.

In the Fetal Position for Safety!

I once read somewhere that when a person is threatened or experiences discouragement they will curl up in a ball for protection and comfort, mimicking the protective safety of their mother's womb. I believe this to be true. But I also believe it is possible to curl up for protection and comfort in more ways than are just physical in nature. I believe it is possible to curl up emotionally and intellectually. How?

- When you fear you curl up and hide intellectually by saying "I just don't want to think about it?"
- When you fear you curl up and shut down emotionally by saying, "Let's talk about something else; it's just too painful to talk about that."
- When you fear you curl up experientially by avoiding challenges that appear to be too hard to overcome.
- Fear can make the strong weak, the smart dumb and the courageous wilt under pressure.
- Fear can transform you into the little lady in the big dark room, isolated, lonely, hurting, and depressed.

52

The reason all of this is important is because when you begin to attempt great things for God you will be threatened. You will be threatened by your own insecurities and you will be challenged by external threats. When these threats come it will make a difference how you confront and overcome them. When you begin to make a difference for God, trouble will show up. Jesus guaranteed it (John 16:33). But be of good cheer. God has overcome your fears. He has offered you a solution to the threats you experience as fear.

Chapter in Review
Questions for Discussion

- What, if anything, can you learn from the "little lady in the big dark room"story? Are you on your way to becoming that type of person?

- What fears do you face that are a threat to your well-being?

    1.

    2.

    3.

- What fears do you face that are a threat to your being?

    1.

    2.

    3.

- By reading 2 Corinthians 7 what can you learn about how even a great man like Paul dealt with his fears and discouragement?

NOT THINKING ABOUT FEAR, IS A STRATEGY
ABOUT FEAR.

IT'S EASY TO BE BRAVE FROM A SAFE DISTANCE.

BE STRONG AND COURAGEOUS! DO NOT BE AFRAID OR
DISCOURAGED, FOR THE LORD YOUR GOD IS WITH YOU
WHEREVER YOU GO!

ATHEIST, HINDU, HUMANIST, OR CHRISTIAN...FEAR
AFFECTS YOU.

CONFRONTATION

Chapter 8

Identifying 7 Common Fears that Matter

did I miss it?; what about me?; you're in my space;
missing the show; looking silly; being wasted; gone for good

Question: If everyone has fear and it functions as a threat to your well-being and to your being (your very person), then how can you rightly identify real fear? Fear comes in many forms. It is helpful to identify several major categories of fear. If the tide of bravery and courage is to rise, fear must be identified with laser-like attention.

7 fears that will keep you from being brave

The fear of nature is what most people think of when they describe their fears. In fact, most fear surveys identify natural or animalistic fears as the top fears that frighten and intimidate us. The fear of animals, of storms, of water, of dogs and spiders and similar kinds of fears are rooted in the mysteries of nature. This may explain why TV shows that feature nature are so popular, especially programs that demonstrate the extreme dangers of nature.

The intimidation you feel during a storm or the nausea you sense when climbing heights or the suffocation you feel when engulfed by water are all rooted in the fear of nature. To be caught in a storm, bitten by a snake or a spider, mangled by a dog or to fall from a great height are all fears rooted responses to the natural world. And since you cannot control nature, your fears of it are exacerbated all the more by the mysteries of nature.

But not all fears are as simple or as obvious as standing on a cliff and overlooking the abyss and fearing that you may fall. Most fears are more complex and sophisticated. In fact, the fears you will deal with in real life have very little to do with things that go "bump in the night" or that scare you because they creep and crawl.

The Fear Killer Generation Remix

The reason it is important for you to identify your fears is because when you begin to do God's will, attempting and accomplishing great things for God, fear and doubt will arise. If you attempt to start a Bible study in your school, fear will cause you to hesitate. If you begin to share the gospel with your friends, fear will show up through their rejection of your testimony.

If you challenge your youth group to really make a difference in your community, fear will arise through the resistance you receive from other believers. If you decide to live a pure and holy life, fear will arise in the form of the rejection you may feel from not going along with the crowd.

Over the next few pages seven significant fears will be identified, along with a brief response as to how the gospel of Jesus Christ impacts each of these fears. So, get a pen and start making notes.

Fear One
did I miss it?

The fears that most of us deal with are much less visible than the fear of nature but are far more deadly and paralyzing, such as the fear of missing "it". This is the silent fear that many people live with. They don't want to miss "it".

It is the dread of living a life without ever figuring out what "it" is or how to get "it." It's the fear you experience when you're not invited to the party, or you're not asked out on the date, to the prom, or when you're left out of what's happening at school. It's the fear of never counting.

This fear is especially important when it comes to doing God's will. There is nothing more disappointing than to know what God wants you to do and then not do it. To miss out on the opportunities God gives is a tragedy.

The failure to figure out the 'meaning of it' all drives many people on a relentless search for meaning and purpose. This is the spiritual dimension of life.

It's like being asked that dreaded question, "What are you going to do once you graduate from high school?" Many people can't answer that question because they don't have a clue. Why? Some will answer, "Because the future is so confusing and if I make a mistake I'll blow my big chance in life. I'll wait and figure out what "it" is and then I'll grow up."

The "it" can be described as happiness, serenity, fulfillment or a sense of purpose and meaning. The failure to figure out the "meaning of it all" drives many people on a relentless search that often ends in failure because it is characterized by fear. This is the spiritual dimension of life.

This is why many people live unfulfilled lives of quiet desperation, a desperation born of the fear that personal happiness, true joy, meaningful relationships, and individual meaning will by-pass them.

Evidence of this fear can be seen in the happy section of any bookstore. Shelf after shelf in the self-help section of most major bookstores are lined with books on how to have a happy life, a happy marriage, a happy attitude at work, and how to search for and discover your purpose in life. You seek this kind of fulfillment. You yearn for it and pursue it at all costs.

Why Do Others Have "It" and I Don't?

What makes the fear of living an unfulfilled life so devastating is that while you are searching for "it", it often appears that others have "it" while you do not. It's the fear that all your friends are happy and you're not; that they have figured "it" out and you haven't.

The fear of not finding the "it" of life combined with the appearance that other people have already found "it", (when, in fact, they probably haven't) can drive you to despair and depression.

And have you ever noticed how the fear of missing "it" causes many people to do stupid things in high school or college just so they'll be in the center of whatever "it" is? Somebody once told me when I was in school, "Never do anything – take drugs, get wasted, have sex – with somebody with whom you will not spend the rest of your life." Good advice, but hard to live by.

Think about how many things you do with people whose relationship with you is only temporary. In fact, I haven't seen many of the people I graduated from high school with since the night of graduation. Then I think of all the stupid things I did simply to show them that "I was the man." Blame it on being young and stupid – it was still produced out of a desire to not miss "it" with my friends.

Jesus is "It!"

When you don't have "it" and you think others do you will end up desiring to live their life instead of living your own for the glory of God. The call to live a fearless life is a call for you to live the life God has for you to live and not the life of someone else.

What would happen if you discovered that the "it" is a relationship with a person, the person of Jesus Christ? What would happen to your fears of missing "it" if you learned that the "it" is a life lived in a dynamic relationship with the very person who loved you and came to give His life for you so that you might find life to the fullest? (John 10:10) You wouldn't have to wish for someone else's life; you could live your own life set free in Jesus Christ.

> When you don't have "it" and you think others do you will end up desiring to live their life instead of living your own for the glory of God. The call to live a fearless life is a call for you to live the life God has for you to live and not the life of someone else.

Fear in Review

Questions for Discussion

- Is the fear of missing "it" a real fear?
- Do you ever fear that you're being left out while others seem to be having all the fun?
- What stupid things am I doing in an effort to find "it?" Are these things harmful?
- Why is it that many refuse to see that Jesus Christ is "it?"

Fear Two
what about me?

But the fear of missing "it" is only part of the equation of fear. **The fear of the "self" is a close companion to the fear of missing "it."** This fear sounds a bit odd, a bit crazy, but it's true. I meet people all the time who have no clue as to who they are and what their life is all about. Why would a person be afraid of the self? It's actually called autophobia – the fear of being alone or of oneself.

The fear of the "self" is the fear of never knowing the nature of your own heart and mind, especially in relation to your past, present, and future. It's the fear of facing the BIG QUESTION – WHO AM I?

Many times when I speak to a group of people – young or old – I'll ask the question, "Who and what are you?" When I ask this question you would think I had just pulled the pin on a hand grenade and thrown it into the crowd. People will squirm, fidget, and become very uncomfortable. Why? Because I have just asked "the" question that gets so close to them that they don't know how to respond.

Me and "It"

The search to know yourself and the search for "it" are closely related to each other. Most people spend an entire life trying to answer questions like: "Who am I?" "What makes me like I am?" "How and why am I different from other people?" "Why do I do what I do?" "Why do I think the way I think?" "What experiences have shaped me?" "Why do I respond the way I do?" "Is who I am good or bad?" "Who are my parents, really?" All of these questions are produced by the fear of never fully comprehending your own identity.

Believe it or not, most people are deathly afraid to take the journey to discover who they are as individuals, why they function the way they do and what it is about them that makes them the way they are.

The uncomfortable feelings of facing a painful past, shaky present, or uncertain future frightens so many people that the vast majority simply go through life as passive reactionaries rather than operate out of a true sense of self that can bring humble confidence to any challenge.

The fear of never discovering the real you is a real fear that stifles personal creativity and fosters the inability to develop and maintain meaningful relationships.

For example – and here's a clue about relationships – how in the world can you know someone else, how to have a relationship with him or her, or whom to marry – unless you know who you are?

To know God is the supreme form of all knowledge. Yet, to live an unconsidered life is a travesty of the highest order. Again, if you don't know who you are how can you expect to know anyone else?

59

And what if you arrive at the answer to the question "Who am I?" without God in the equation? This is what throws many people over the edge – the fear of never truly knowing one's purpose. For example, some very famous people in movie history had a difficult time in discovering who they were and then living to tell about:

- Peg Entwhistle (1908 – 1932) She was a beautiful rising silent film star, but was struck by the fear of a lack of self-identity. At the age of 23 she dove headfirst off the letter "H" of the famous Hollywood sign in LA. In her suicide note she wrote, "I'm afraid I'm a coward. I'm sorry for everything."
- George Reeves (1922 – 1959) You may have seen him in those old black and white (and later, colored) episodes of the TV Superman series. Reeves committed suicide when he learned he couldn't separate who he was in person from his TV persona.
- Judy Garland (1922 – 1969) Star of the Wizard of Oz and mother of actress Liza Minelli, overdosed on drugs even though she was one of the top stars of Hollywood at the time.
- Marilyn Monroe (1926 – 1962) Hollywood beauty and friend of powerful presidents and famous actors overdosed on drugs.
- John Belushi (1949 – 1982) Star of "Animal House" and Saturday Night Live overdosed on drugs trying to keep up the highs he got from acting but that he couldn't maintain.
- Marguaux Hemingway (1954 – 1996) A gorgeous supermodel who committed suicide on July 2nd, 1996, the anniversary of the suicide of her famous grandfather, Ernest Hemingway.
- Kurk Cobain (1967 – 1994) Cobain, genius musician and founder of the band Nirvana, committed suicide with a shot to the head. High on cocaine, Cobain died estranged from many of his friends, even though wildly successful and incredibly rich.
- Heath Ledger (1979 – 2008) A mesmerizing actor and big screen star who wowed fans with his eerily sardonic portrayal of the Joker in the '08 release of Batman movie. He overdosed on drugs just prior to the release of Batman: The Dark Knight.

But what about all the non-famous people who never figure "it" out either? Their names are not in the newspapers and they don't make the evening news. But they are nonetheless tormented by the dreaded fear of never knowing who they are as an individual and never knowing their purpose in life.

Jesus and Me!

What would happen to the threat you feel when you go on the journey of self-discovery if you knew that your true self could be found in Jesus Christ? If there were ever a person who had the ability to get into the head and hearts of people it was Jesus.

Just ask the woman of Samaria who met Jesus, the fear killer, at Jacob's well in the heat of the midday sun (John 4). Jesus asked her such personal and piercing questions that it is no wonder she told Jesus, "**Sir, I perceive that you are a prophet**." In fact, she later told her entire village, "**Come, see a man who told me all that I ever did**."

Did Jesus really tell her everything she ever did? Not according to Scripture. What Jesus did was to look into her soul and define who she was in her current lifestyle so that she felt like He had exposed the secrets of her life. He then told her that she could have a new life, a new identity in Him. He told her how she could be different by receiving the living water of eternal life.

And what was the result? She changed from being a woman afraid to visit the watering well when others would be there to a woman willing to evangelize her entire town. Incredible!

There is one truth about those who live brave and fearless lives. They are continually discovering who they are in Jesus Christ. If you allow Jesus Christ to kill the fear in you of self-discovery, then you will no longer be defined completely by your family heritage, the mistakes you've made, or what your friends say about you. You will be defined by what it means to be "in Christ." (2 Corinthians 5:17)

Fear in Review
Questions for Discussion

- When you think about yourself, how do you define who you are?
- Is it often painful to ask such personal questions?
- Who have you allowed to define who you are?
- What events, good or bad, give definition to who you are?
- What does it mean to be 'in Christ'? How can this help us in the process of self-discovery?

Fear Three
you're in my space

Most of us have a Facebook or MySpace page. We post all kinds of information about ourselves on these web pages - comments, pictures, ideas, invitations. Internet pages like this are emotionally safe because you don't see the people you're talking to face to face. They don't see the zit on your forehead or your awkwardness in how you speak or walk. This kind of cyber-relationship is safe.

This is why personal encounters with others can freak you out. So, have you ever met a person that was fidgety around you? They wouldn't look at you face to face. And no matter what you tried they wouldn't warm up to you? The fear of never understanding who you are merges into the "fear of others.'"

It is called androphobia or arrhenphobia – the fear of other humans. This is the fear of relationships, of personal intimacy or of finding and participating in long-lasting meaningful friendships.

It is this fear that is in the background of the friction that sometimes exists at school among you and your friends. It exists in marriages, among siblings, with

co-workers, and with people in general.

Think about it. If you have a person who doesn't know the "it" of life, who has no clue as to who they are as a person (and throw in a little phobia here and there), then you will have a very unhappy, fearful person who is probably unable or unwilling to develop meaningful, productive relationships.

So, You're Afraid of Being Burned by Others

I meet so many people who are afraid of relationships for fear of being "burned," (to be taken advantage of). These are what I call the "poker player" people – no emotion, no connection. They refuse to show their emotional and intellectual cards to anybody and often have a blank stare on their face.

The thought of taking a risk that may lead to personal injury is unthinkable. They may have seen their parents burned by love or a friend disappointed in a relationship and the end result is a fear of relational intimacy or personal transparency.

Think a little deeper about this fear for a moment. How many of your friends have you known who refuse to open up and engage in meaningful conversations or, when they do talk, it's all bluster and arrogance as they protect themselves from being too personal.

"But the fear of others is not just about intimacy, it's also about intimidation, as well. The number of people who function out of fear when it comes to their relationships with others hinges on the intimidation factor. Like the school bully who bluffs the other kids in the class with his brashness and bravado, the desire to be approved of by others bullies us into a fearful, whippish existence that keeps us from acting with courage and confidence."

Think about it. If you have a person who doesn't know the "it" of life, who has no clue as to who they are as a person (and throw in a little phobia here and there), then you will have a very unhappy, fearful person who is probably unable or unwilling to develop meaningful, productive relationships.

And it's not just with you and your friends. What about your parents? How many families do not talk and when they do it's all yell and no conversation. How many marriages have been corrupted or broken because at least one of the spouses had unresolved, unrequited fears? Such fears can be devastating.

It's what causes some students in your school to go through their entire high school experience and never really know anybody.

The fear of others is what may cause you or your friends to attempt reckless and irresponsible behavior for fear that if you do not try them you won't be accepted in the crowd. It's the false shame of saying no to a boyfriend pressing for sexual favors for fear that he will think you a prude. And the list goes on.

Fear can become so pervasive in your relationships that it can motivate you to lie to those you love, become disloyal when commitment is called for, and to walk away from relationships when they become difficult.

I Don't Want to Be Bullied

But the fear of others is not just about intimacy; it's about intimidation as well. The number of people who live in fear when it comes to their relationships often times hinges on the intimidation factor. Like the school bully who bluffs the other kids in the class with his brashness and bravado, the desire to be approved of by others bullies you into a fearful, whippish existence that will keep you from acting with courage and confidence.

The anxiety that comes from seeking the approval of others can be stifling to your creativity and your willingness to take risks. You may fear the ridicule of others – catagelphobia – to the degree that you fail to function as an authentic human being.

Jesus and the Courage to Love

What would happen if you were set free to love (Romans 13:8-10)? What would happen if you had the boldness to love others even if it meant you might be disappointed in the outcomes?

I can hear the protest now: "But what if I get burned?" I usually tell people that it is better to love and get burned than to never love at all. By the way, if you do decide to radically follow Jesus you will get burned. It hurts. But join the company of the committed. Jesus was burned all the way to the cross – and it ended up being the very path through which God would save the very people who burned Him. The "burned" saved the ones who "burned" Him (2 Corinthians 5:19).

If Jesus sets you free to love, to relate, to build friendships that are life-changing, it could change your home, your school, and your church. The truth of the gospel is that Jesus Christ came to put His life in you and to live His life through you in loving relationships. This means that you can freely love others because you have been set free to love in Jesus Christ.

Fear in Review

Questions for Discussion

- What kind of a friend are you?
- Do you fear relationships? Or, do you embrace new opportunities to get to know other people?
- What would happen if you became fearless and bold in building new, Christ-centered relationships?
- Is your youth group a friendly youth group? Is it open to those not involved in your church?

Fear Four
did I miss the show?

I hate to be late for an event. I feel like if I walk in late and miss the first few moments of a movie or a show I have missed the "set up" – the most important part of the event that will explain the rest of the event.

I have a friend who is unable to make decisions. He has what I call "decisional constipation" (pardon the grossness of this term). He just can't get things moving when it comes to making decisions.

He suffers from the fear of missed opportunities. His thinking works like this - if he chooses opportunity A he fears he will miss opportunity B. Every decision he makes means that if he chooses one thing he will not be able to do the other thing.

I remember one occasion when we decided to eat lunch together. The agonizing process of deciding where to eat was excruciating. After thirty minutes of discussing the pros and cons of different places to eat we finally made a decision that he later appeared to regret because he complained the entire time we dined.

I didn't care. All I knew was that I was so hungry that I was ready to start gnawing on my own leg.

The Many Forms of Fear
1. **Fear of missing "it" – I just don't get what life is about!**
2. **Fear of self-discovery – what's my identity?**
3. **Fear of others – can we all really get along?**
4. **Fear of missed opportunities – the door opened and I didn't walk through**
5. **Fear of taking risks – I'd rather play it safe!**
6. **Fear of a wasted life – does my life mean anything to anybody?**
7. **Fear of dying – is this all there is? And is that the end?**

The fear of missed opportunities is a real fear. This fear has two sides. The one side takes place on the front end of the decision-making process when confronted by various and maybe even numerous opportunities. The fear of making a wrong decision paralyzes a person from making any decision at all - decidophobia.

You Need to Decide Now!
This may be one reason why young adults are delaying marriage and a career more than ever. They're afraid of choosing the wrong mate or the wrong career. And while it is true that there are more choices about more things than ever before – careers, jobs, ideas, places to eat, doctors, schools, sports – it's also true that indecision is a real problem. The fear of making a wrong decision literally paralyzes many people from acting at all.

Remember, no decision is a decision. Choosing not to decide is as good as making a decision, right or wrong. If you say "I don't want to think about it" you are saying, whether you know it or not, "I will not decide in this matter." This kind of indecision is deadly.

The other side of this fear takes place on the back end of life or an event. As your choices in life are reviewed the missed opportunities accumulate into a snowball of regret – a sense of regret that may be attributed to the fears that inhibited bold action throughout a lifetime.

The obvious glare of missed opportunities turns into dread and anxiety. No fear may be more sinister than the deep sense of regret you may experience from missed opportunities, when there's no time left to change, alter or relive the decisive moments of life.

The good news is that Jesus Christ has set you free to boldly choose. Secure in Him, you can choose the daring and the risky for His glory. It's time for you to choose Him because He has already chosen you. This is great news. But time is urgent, so choose today (Joshua 24:15).

Fear in Review
Questions for Discussion
- What issues are you facing that require you to make a decision so that you won't miss a God-given opportunity?
- Ask yourself, "How do I make a decision? Do I pray before deciding? Do I consult God's Word? Do I consult trusted friends? Do I listen to the wise counsel of my elders?"
- If you refuse to make a choice now, whom and what will suffer?

Fear Five
looking silly?

You might be saying at this point "OK, so let's say I try to get involved and it fails? Won't I look like a fool?" Yes, you may look like a fool because even if you do choose to do the right thing it may be accompanied by **the fear of failing or of taking risks** – atychiphobia. The fear of failing at something will keep you from trying anything. And who wants to look silly if something fails?

The "try factor" in you is diminished or even eliminated when anxiety and worry dominates your heart and mind. Why try if you know you will fail? **The crazy thing about this fear is that you're basing a decision on an unknown**. While the success of any endeavor is an unknown, so is failure.

My parents used to say two things to me when I was afraid to try something for fear of failure – "can't never did" *and* "how do you know if you'll fail or succeed until you've tried?" It was this kind of encouragement that challenged me to try things that I probably would have never tried, fail or not.

Being a part of the fear killer generation is a call to try, to risk, to trust even

65

if it means failure. God may want you to start a Bible study or a prayer group at your school. He may want you to build a relationship with people outside your normal group of friends. No matter what it is, there is always the risk of failure as well as success. Those who are secure in Jesus Christ are willing to risk anything for Him. But how will you know unless you try?

But along with the fear of looking for "it" in life and never finding "it" is the real fear that we will have wasted our life doing things that were unproductive and without meaning or significance.

Fear in Review
Questions for Discussion

- Have you ever missed an opportunity that you wish now you had tried?
- If you knew you would never fail, what would you do right now?
- Does it help to redefine success not in terms of failure or success, but in terms of obedience?
- Spiritually speaking, many of the things God desires for us to do may seem to bear little fruit at first. Unlike worldly successes that are more immediate, what would happen if we left the results up to God and did whatever he wanted us to do?

Fear Six
on being wasted?

Have you ever been sitting around talking to some of your friends about another friend's troubles and one of you said, "Man, what a waste?" We all have. You will say it about your friends, your family members, and people you see in the news. Why do we say this? We say it because we are acknowledging that that person had great potential but wasted it in some way.

The avalanche of fears that I have mentioned often culminate in a sense that you have wasted or are wasting your life. **The fear of a wasted life** is so deep that it often doesn't surface until tragedy strikes and you take the time to examine the meaning of your life. After a tragedy you will often make resolutions to live a more meaningful, purposeful life that fades as each day passes. It may not even take a tragedy to stir within you a sense of anxiety over the "lost years."

What a Waste
I'll never forget what happened the month after I graduated from high school. One of the girls in my class had just signed a "letter of intent" to play basketball for a college near our hometown. She had great talent and was well liked. The possibilities were limitless.

But what did she do? She got wasted on the night of July 4th and then got on a motorcycle (without a working headlight) with her boyfriend at about 2 a.m. on

July 5th. They crossed over a railroad track and hit their best friend head-on as he drove over the tracks from the opposite direction. Both she and her boyfriend were killed on impact. I'll never forget what her coach said in anger: "What a waste."

There are too many wasted lives in this world and most of them are not wasted in a car accident. Most lives are wasted by living average, risk-less lives where the same old humdrum, day-to-day mindset kills any willingness to be brave and bold.

It reminds me of the man who told me that he had finally discovered what he should be doing with his life, though he was in his sixties. His comment was, "It's a shame that we find these things out too late." How true.

Most live from day to day trying to make the best of each day. But along with the fear of looking for "it" in life and never finding "it" is the real fear that you will have wasted your life doing things that were unproductive and without meaning or significance. It can be argued that this fear is so deep that it is difficult to articulate.

Jesus on the Wasted Life

Do you know what the fear killer said about a wasted life? Jesus said in Matthew 12:39, "**Whoever finds his life will lose it, and whoever loses his life for my sake will find it.**" This same kind of principle of losing and finding is stated in Matthew 16:24-28. Don't miss the truth of what Jesus said. If you spend your life trying to protect your life, keep free from risk, from failure, from commitment to a great cause, you will waste your life.

But if you give your life away to the person of Jesus Christ you will find it. Your life will not have been wasted. A life committed to Jesus Christ is never a waste.

Fear in Review
Questions for Discussion

- Is the fear of wasting your life causing you to waste your life?
- Laziness, unconcern and indifference are all indicators of a wasted life; what are the indicators of a person who is not wasting their life for God?
  1.

  2.

  3.

  4.

Fear Seven
gone for good?

So, let's talk about the final fear, the fear that starts with the letter "D", you know, DEATH. Before you freak out on me, stop for a minute. You may think you're invincible now, but in the back of your mind you know the big "D" is coming. Even the Word of God affirms that all of us have a date with death (Hebrews 9:27-28).

Adults find it hard to believe that students like you live a two-fold life – they think you think you're invincible, and that you never think about death and dying. But you do think about death. This is why all the previously mentioned fears play out against the backdrop of the ultimate fear, **the fear of death and dying**. Intuitively and instinctively you know death is coming.

Death is the backdrop against which life is lived. It's the dirty little secret that everyone knows but no one is talking about. And while you don't always talk about it, death is the only certainty toward which all of us are headed.

Occasionally, something will happen that will bring the inevitably of death into sharp perspective. A high school friend of yours will die in a car wreck or a terrible disaster will occur and scare you to almost insanity. Most of the time, however, you suppress the notion of death. Death is the ultimate fear, so you don't like to think about it, even though you do. Questions like "When will I die?" "How will I die?" "What happens to me after I die?" will not go away or leave you alone.

It must be stated that next to the fear of death, is another unspoken fear – a death that takes place before dying. It is the death of self, the death of hope, the death of a future, the death of possibility and potential. Fear and cowardice can build into your psyche a fear of dying before you die. It's not the fear of how you will die or even of the physical nature of death. It is the fear of death that comes from having never lived at all.

Jesus and Death

So, if death is the ultimate fear, then what did Jesus say about death? He said many things about death. One of the things He said about death He said at the funeral service of one of His best friends, Lazarus (John 11).

Confronted by the sorrow of Mary and Martha, Lazarus' sisters, Jesus said the most amazing thing prior to raising Lazarus from the dead. (John 11:25-26), "**I am the resurrection and the life. Whoever believes in me, though he die, yet shall he live, and everyone who lives and believes in me shall never die. Do you believe this?**"

This is amazing. Jesus raised Lazarus from the dead to give you insight into the truth that not even death is a problem for Him and His followers. While on earth Jesus did not raise every person from the dead, but He raised enough people from the dead to demonstrate that not even death wins.

So, here's the deal. If you are in Jesus Christ and Jesus Christ is in you then you don't have to be afraid of death. You will be able to say with the Apostle Paul (1 Corinthians 15:54-57), "**Death is swallowed up in victory. O death, where is your victory? O death, where is your sting? The sting of death is sin, and the power of sin is the law. But thanks be to God, who gives us the victory through our Lord Jesus Christ.**"

In Jesus Christ God has announced the death of death in the death and resurrection of Jesus Christ. This is good news for those who are in Jesus Christ.

Fear in Review
Questions for Discussion

- What would happen to you right now if you died? Heaven? Hell?

- Are you the kind of person who likes to play it safe? Why?

- How many opportunities would take advantage of for God – mission trips, ministry – if you didn't have to worry about what ultimately happens?

Chapter 9

Transition – Is a Fear-Less Life Possible?

After reading this list of fears you're probably wondering if a fearless life is even possible. Fear can rule a person's life. From the common phobias of nature, to the fear of missing "it", of not discovering ourselves, to being in relationship with others, to the fear of wasting a lifetime only to die unfulfilled, fear can overwhelm you, stifle your creative abilities, ruin your confidence to be a complete person with significant, meaningful relationships.

The question remains: Can fear be overcome? Can the fears that seek to kill you be killed? Is it possible to live fear-free life or a life of less fear? A life of less fear is possible. But it won't be easy. It will call for you to confront what may be some very vulnerable and painful areas of your life. But there is hope. Jesus is more than able to dismantle every fear.

The Chapter in Review
Questions for Discussion

- Can you remember and list the seven fears mentioned in the last chapter?

1.

2.

3.

4.

5.

6.

7.

- Of the 7 fears, which fear dominates my thinking the most?

- Groups have personalities just like people do. What fear or fears most characterize the youth ministry of my church or the church altogether?

- Is a fear-less life possible? Or is it a fairy tale?

Chapter 10

How Fear Works

barriers, boundaries, bondage, baggage

This is a dangerous chapter because it asks the questions that may be threatening to your ego and risky in that it will challenge you to take action that is courageous and brave. If you're to be a part of the fear killer generation you must understand how fear works. A personal example is in order.

Scared to Death by a Storm

I do not consider myself to be a fearful person, that is, until a storm hits. It was a surreal experience of fear and dread combined. On the night of February 5, 2008 multiple tornadoes – the most in recorded history in winter time – passed through "tornado alley," stretching from Arkansas, through southern Missouri, western and central Kentucky, and western and central Tennessee, killing fifty plus people, and destroying millions of dollars in personal and public property.

The storm frightened thousands of people as they spent a sleepless night in their "safe places," listening to the piercing sounds of the storm sirens and watching or listening to the weather station. One storm after another passed through with the force that only nature can bring to bear on buildings, homes, and lives.

What was so surreal about this evening of storms was that my son and I were in a Minneapolis hotel attending a conference for fathers and sons, far out of reach of the storms. I watched helplessly on a computer radar screen as the storms passed through one by one, all the while communicating by cell phone with my wife and daughter as they spent most of the night in the hallway bathroom.

It was like watching someone you love get beat up right in front of your eyes, yet not being able to do a single thing about it. It was a fear that all four of us had not felt in a long time. It was the fear of being helpless, unable, incapable, fragile, and small.

We were all scared – my wife and daughter were scared because they were in the storm, praying audibly as they helplessly waited for each storm to pass. My

How ironic! There was the fear of being in the storm and there was the fear of not being in the storm – a feeling of not wanting to be where one was and the feeling of wanting to be in the storm to help. Crazy!

son and I were scared because we were watching helplessly from a distance without the slightest ability to do anything at all to help those we love.

How ironic! There was the fear of being in the storm and there was the fear of not being in the storm – a feeling of not wanting to be where we were; of wanting to be in the storm to help. Crazy!

This is the nature of fear. It strikes at the heart of every human being in strange and mysterious ways. What is fear? How does it function in our lives? Where does it come from? And, more importantly, how can fear be overcome?

Gut-Wrenching Fear

There is no doubt that fear elicits gut-wrenching, heartbreaking emotion. The word itself stirs up what are often deeply disturbing and interpersonal anxieties that are thought to be better left unsaid. Fear takes you to your high school days where you were (maybe still are) petrified at the thought of a first date, or of your part in the school play. More importantly, fear awakens the dreaded anxiety of not being accepted or of not becoming a meaningful part of school life.

8th Grade

My own mind is taken back to my eighth grade year when my family moved from Kentucky to Missouri. I had been telling my friends that I would not be returning after the Christmas break, but everyone just shrugged it off. I had been around for so long that everyone thought it inconceivable that I would permanently leave. There was no send-off party, no fanfare. My self-esteem took a blow at the lack of sympathy concerning my departure.

The semester ended and we moved. Knots formed in my stomach for two weeks as I awaited the beginning of a new semester at a new school in a new state. It turned out to be the best move we ever made as a family, but the fear and dread of that move is still palpable some 30 years later.

So, ask your friends what they most fear and you will get a litany of fears that lie just beneath the surface of everyday life – family fears, economic fears, relational anxieties, marital worries, employment concerns, parental angst – and the list goes on. Fear transcends race, culture, creed and social pedigree. It is a common feature of all people in all nations on every continent on the face of the earth.

Fear knows no boundaries.

- It invades the hearts and minds of the down and the out and the up and the in.
- Fear walks the hallways of politics and power affecting all who become contaminated by its infection – it's in the hearts of your friends.
- It visits schools, homes, work cubicles, college dorm rooms, class rooms, nursing homes, airplanes, hospitals, board rooms, and the local coffee shops.
- It visits the subway of the lonely and the outcast, the helpless, and the homeless and the ivory towers of the powerful and the potent.
  While fear may express itself in differing forms in different people in different ways, it is fear nonetheless.
  Mention the word fear and all kinds of images and experiences come to

mind. Fears from the past and the present flood your mind with waves of dread, anxiety, worries and embarrassment. Fear drowns your hopes, squelches your courage, and stifles your God-given creativity.

The caged animal

I love visiting zoos. Zoos give me the opportunity to see animals that I would not otherwise be able to see. Visiting a zoo is exhilarating. But visiting a zoo also gives me a sense of sadness. Watching beautiful animals pace back and forth in small cages reminds me that God made these animals to be free.

Fear is like the cage at a zoo. God intended for you to be free to love and serve Him (John 8:32). But fear, produced in you by sin, cages you in. As a result you become caged, confined, and contained. Like a caged animal, you pace back and forth desiring the freedom of the "out there", of the "yet to be experienced", of the new, but unwilling and unable to break out of the confining fears that imprison and paralyze you.

Fear may be the one thing that keeps you from the freedom you desire and the destiny you long for. Why? Because by its very nature fear is a thief that will rob you of the courage to try new things, to take risks that bring great reward, and to dream large dreams that have significance and meaning.

Fear as a Barrier

Have you ever wanted something so bad that you could taste it, feel it, see it coming, but were afraid to go for it? It's like there is something between you and the thing you want.

As a barrier, it's what keeps a person 'in' rather than allowing them to face the 'out there' of an unknown, but exciting future. Fear keeps you from living in forward."

Fear acts as a barrier, an unseen, insurmountable wall. Fear is what comes between you and the very things you desire. It's the feeling of not being able to do something because you're being blocked by an unseen force.

Like the Great Wall of China that at one time served as a barrier between a protected world and the threats to that world, fear rises up in you like a great wall that keeps you from what lies on the other side. It's what keeps you from meaningful relationships. It's what keeps parents and children from meaningful communication. It's what keeps you from your friends. It's what keeps spouses from reconciling.

Fear keeps races and classes of people separate and suspicious of each other. It's what keeps nations from moving toward peaceful negotiations and it's what keeps co-workers from working out peaceful solutions.

It's what keeps you from trying something new. It's what keeps you from attempting anything different or novel that may appear to be a threat to your sense of security or well-being.

Most important, fear is what comes between you and what you want to do, what you need to do. And it's what between you and your dreams. Fear is what paralyzes you from acting bravely and choosing wisely. As a barrier, it's what keeps you "in" or "on the other side" rather than allowing you to face the "out there" or the "over there" of an unknown but exciting future. Fear keeps you from living in forward.

The good news of the gospel is that in Jesus Christ God has broken down the barriers between God and sinners and between sinners and sinners – in Jesus Christ the barrier that existed between you and God has been torn down enabling you to have a freedom to live and love for Him.

Ephesians 2:14-16 says it best: **"For He himself is our peace, who has made us both one and has broken down in his flesh the dividing wall of hostility by abolishing the law of commandments expressed in ordinances, that He might create in Himself one new man in place of the two, so making peace, and might reconcile us both to God in one body through the cross, thereby killing the hostility."** Jesus, as the fear killer, breaks down the barriers that come between you and your freedom. And if He sets you free you will be truly free.

Fear as a Boundary

And what about all those rules? Don't rules drive you crazy? Rules at school, rules in class, rules at home, rules for driving – rules, rules, rules. Don't rules mean limited freedom? Most rules are good, but some aren't. The rules fear will set for you mean false boundaries have been set for you.

So, if fear functions as a barrier it also acts as a *boundary*. Feel like you're shut in and locked up? It's fear. As a boundary, fear will cause you to set pre-determined limits on yourself before you even try. How many people do you hear say, "I'm afraid I can't do that?" You may say such things before you even try because you are bound by your fears.

Your fears are like ruts in the road of life that were made by previous travelers, but that have kept us on the road of the familiar and the routine.

It's the reason you don't try out for the school play or the reason your mom doesn't fill out an application to return to college after having been out of school for some years. It's what sets limits on your desire to achieve or to take advantage of new and risky opportunities. You will jokingly say, "I don't see myself doing that" as a way of cloaking the boundaries you have allowed fear to set for you.

Your fears are like ruts in the road of life that were made by previous travelers, but that keep you on the road of the familiar and the routine. Fear is what boxes you in to the mundane and the minimal. Fear forms boundaries around you that isolate you from others, squelches your creativity, and minimizes your bravery, and wastes your abilities.

The Electric Fence

As a boundary, fear is like the underground electric fence you can purchase to control your dog or your cat. A battery controlled collar is placed on the animal. An electrically charged fence line

And the baggage of fear doesn't get any lighter as the years pass. Unresolved fears become heavier and more cumbersome as time passes.

is buried beneath the surface of the yard at a predetermined distance that gives the animal enough room to roam, but not without boundaries.

Each time the animal approaches the fence an electrical charge is set off in the collar and the animal backs down from crossing the unseen barrier for fear of the pain. Talk about a "pain in the neck."

What is deceptive about this underground electric fence is that there are no visible fence posts or guardrails, just the pain that comes from approaching a pre-determined boundary. This kind of system gives the illusion of freedom, but it is a bounded, pre-determined freedom, which is no freedom at all. The animal is conditioned to the point that after some time, even when the fence is not electrically charged, it will not roam beyond the limits of the buried fence.

Fear functions like this underground electric fence. No matter the fear, it acts as a boundary so that each time you're tempted to venture off on a new course of action fear shocks you into inaction.

The fears buried beneath the surface keep you from a destiny of creativity and purpose. The pain caused by your fears temper your courage to overcome the boundaries of fear. The illusion of freedom comes from the unseen, below-the-surface stuff that frightens you, stifling your abilities and robbing you of a future of possibility and promise. The consequences are devastating. Over time fear conditions you not to press the boundaries of life. New adventures are out and sameness is in.

Fear as Bondage

The barrier-like separation and the boundary-setting limitations of fear are only part of its destructive nature. Fear also functions as bondage. Fear functions like shackles that bind you and inhibit your emotional, intellectual, and even physical movements. Fear is like a set of handcuffs that stifle your creativity.

Fear inhibits, imprisons, quarantines, and corners you into a life of spiritual and psychological bondage that is not easily broken. And once fear binds you, your life becomes small and insignificant. The will to act is corrupted and the desire to dare is confiscated by fear. Fear can become so limiting that it not only places you in your own maximum security prison, but in solitary confinement as well.

Jesus declared that God sent Him to set free those in bondage (Luke 4:18). It's truth that sets people free (John 8:32). Since Jesus Christ is truth (John 14:6), He is able to set you free from bondage that may express itself in bondage to pride, selfishness, and self-loathing.

Fear as Baggage

The weight of fear feels like the weight of the world. The cumulative effect of fear is that your attitudes and behaviors become lethargic and cumbersome. Experiencing the baggage of fear is like running through an airport when you're late for a flight, knowing that you're going to miss your flight. Instead of running free and unencumbered to board a flight that will take you "out of here" you're dragging several pieces of heavy luggage that weigh you down.

And the baggage of fear doesn't get any lighter as the years pass. Unresolved fears become heavier and more cumbersome as time passes. The baggage of fear weighs some people down so much that they become dysfunctional. I once heard about a lady so fearful of being with people and of engaging the outside world that she found it nearly impossible to leave the safe confines of her house and walk to the end of her driveway to get the morning newspaper. Just imagine that – the weight of fear was so heavy that it rendered this woman incapable of the simplest of tasks.

Have you allowed fear to become the barrier, the boundary, the bondage, and/or the baggage that weighs you down? Jesus has come to set you free. Jesus has come to take your burden and to give you a burden that you should carry, that you can carry (**Matthew 11:28-30**): "Come to me, all who labor and are heavy laden, and I will give you rest. Take my yoke upon you, and learn from me, for I am gentle and lowly in heart, and you will find rest for your souls. For my yoke is easy, and my burden is light." Rather than carry around a load of fear, Jesus has come to give you a burden of purpose and meaning, a burden that will give rest to your weary, fear-filled soul.

To be brave can be defined as possessing or displaying boldness, valor, fearlessness, daring or courage. In essence, bravery is the outward expression of an inward heart of courage – if you have courage you will act bravely. Bravery is courage in action.

Chapter in Review
Questions for Discussion
- What are the four aspects of how fear works?

- Which particular aspect do you deal with the most?

Chapter 11

What Fear Does
insulation, isolation, inaction

This is where I'm going to ask you to think. Let's unpack a rather challenging series of statements: Fear can neutralize you. Fear can paralyze your bravery. What in the world does this mean? How does fear neutralize courage? What does it mean to have your sense of bravery paralyzed by fear?

To Be Courageous

Courage is defined by the '04 *Oxford American Writer's Thesaurus* as what makes someone capable of facing extreme danger and difficulty without retreating. It implies not only bravery and a dauntless spirit but the ability to endure in times of adversity.

Courage is a state or quality of mind and spirit that enables you to face danger with self-possession, confidence, and resolution. Words like guts, fortitude, resolution, tenacity, and nerve are comparable to the word courage. Fear neutralizes every dimension of courage by attacking the will to face head-on that which stands in the way of the desire to attempt that which must be accomplished.

To Be Brave

To be brave can be defined as possessing or displaying boldness, valor, fearlessness, daring or courage. In essence, bravery is the outward expression of an inward heart of courage – if you have courage you will act bravely. Bravery is courage in action.

Yet, this is where fear raises its ugly head. As fear attacks your courage it in turn paralyzes your willingness to act bravely. If courage is destroyed and dismantled your ability to function bravely becomes incapacitated.

The consequences of fear are devastating. As your courage and bravery diminish two specific things happen. Fear erects a barrier between you and the very things you desire to do. This fear barrier keeps you from the good you desire.

You desire to ask a girl out on a date but cower at the thought for fear that you will lose your nerve and ultimately be rejected even before you've acted. And the examples could go on forever. Name a goal and then just see what happens as you move toward that goal – fear will attack your courage, squelch your bravery, and end up stifling your progression in life.

The by-products of fear are always devastating and destructive. Interestingly enough, fear produces the very things that cause fear. This is the vicious cycle of fear. Fear produces increased fear and so the story goes.

Trying the Hard Things

For example, if you have a fear of failure that then produces inaction you will continue to live in a state of inaction and thereby continue to experience feelings of failure. In other words, the fearful person fails before he has even tried. So, trying the hard things is never easy because fear will always be there.

The devastating consequences of fear are deadly. No other factor in life is as inhibiting as fear. Fear stifles creativity, stops personal growth, excludes risk, and renders a person inept. Fear will impact you in at least three areas of life related to personal courage and bravery: *personal insulation*, *relational isolation*, and *creative inaction*.

Fear as Personal Insulation

Personal insulation is living life alone, closed up to others and to new experiences. The consequence is a "morbid introspection" that is over the top and self-centered. It produces those people you know who constantly over-analyze everything and moan and complain about everything.

Fear will make you self-conscious to the degree that every time you walk into a room, open your mouth to say a word, or make a decision, you think everyone is either looking at you or evaluating your every move as a failure.

This is why you may insulate yourself from meaningful relationships and individual risk. The result is that you will become a hyper-introvert, living in a self-contained world produced by fear. This type of "morbid introspection" will make you selfish, self-conscious, and self-absorbed.

Fear as Personal Isolation

But the insulating effect of fear is not the only consequence produced by the lack of courage and bravery. Relational isolation is the consequence that inhibits meaningful personal relationships and intimacy. Though you live in a "connected world" you are, in many ways, more disconnected because of fear.

If you are all about yourself then it makes it very difficult to develop meaningful relationships with others. You will end up living a "texted" life where you communicate with others in a type of short-hand, without having to live face to face with others.

Your world is a MySpace, Facebook type of world where everyone knows something about you but nothing about you. Your generation is the most personally connected, disconnected world in the history of humanity. You can talk to someone on the other side of the world but find it difficult to talk to someone on the other side of the table.

I remember enjoying a meal at a restaurant one day watching a father and son eat together (or at least I thought they were eating together). The father talked on his cell phone the entire time, while the son was head-down "texting" some non-present friend. I'll give it to them for at least being at the same table, but beyond that it appeared that there was a breakdown in their personal relationship.

Relationships are costly. They will pull out of you time, energy, and emotional and intellectual effort. When you become personally insulated, you are more prone to be isolated from meaningful relationships. If it's not about you, or if it threatens you and your security, fear-produced world, it's not real.

Relationships are costly. They will pull out of you time, energy, and emotional and intellectual effort. When you become personally insulated, you are more prone to be isolated from meaningful relationships. If it's not about you, or if it threatens you and your security, fear-produced world, it's not real.

Fear as Creative Inaction

Creative inaction is the long-term product of fear. God has created you to be creative, innovative, and productive. This is what Genesis 1:28 means when it says, **"And God blessed them. And God said to them, 'Be fruitful and multiply and fill the earth and subdue it and have dominion over the fish of the sea and over the birds of the heavens and over every living thing that moves on the earth.'"**

God's purpose for you is more than producing school papers, material products, or producing a touchdown in a football game. God's purpose for you is to creatively engage the world so that your creativity is a reflection of the nature and purpose of your Creator God. Fear as sin, selfishness, and self-absorption actually stifles creativity because it inhibits your free interaction with others and with God's creation that gives birth to your "creative juices." Creative inaction leads to a lack of boldness to try the new, the innovative, or to not act at all.

The Summary

I meet so many students who are disconnected, isolated, and uncreative. When I try to figure out why these three issues characterize the lives of so many students, I will invariably see the issue of fear playing a major role in killing what God wants to do. It's time that you were set free from your isolated, unsulated, uncreative life. This is possible in Jesus Christ.

Chapter in Review
Questions for Discussion

- What happens when you become insulated in how you live and relate?
- Are you the "invisible person," isolated from action?
- What creative purposes and talents has God placed in you?

Chapter 12

The Fear of Peer Pressure – Sarah's Story

What you are about to read is a true story. It serves as an example of what happens when fear wins the day. Theory is one thing, but reality is another. So, read with grace and understanding.

Peer pressure. It's nothing new. It's been around since the beginning of time. Peer pressure is one person convincing another person to do something which, most of the time, is the wrong thing, the stupid thing, or the destructive thing. So, while there is such a thing as "positive peer pressure", too often the pressure is not positive. Just ask Sarah.

Sarah the Beautiful
Sarah was a beautiful 17 year old girl who lived in the community where I pastored. She was smart, pretty, and fairly popular. She appeared level-headed. She was a leader in her school.

Sarah had big plans for her life. She was going to graduate with honors and dump her sleepy little hometown for a bigger and better life. She was not the type of person that would find herself ten years down the road working as a cashier at the local dollar store.

She had plans to accomplish something no one in her family had ever accomplished – to graduate from college, get a good job, do something meaningful, and productive with her life. That is, until she went to "the party".

The Party from Hell
During her senior year Sarah was invited to "the party" of all parties. And get this. The party was hosted by a mom and dad who invited the entire high school student body to their home, bought several kegs of beer, and then left for the evening. They reasoned that the students were going to get drunk anyway so why not have the party at a safe place where parents would at least know where their children were, and they wouldn't have to drive while intoxicated. It was a planned all-nighter.

Sarah wasn't much of a party girl or drinker. She later told me she hated

the taste of beer. But she went anyway just to be a part of all that takes place in the final year of school – parties, proms, and too often promiscuity.

The party was fairly mild at first until one of Sarah's classmates started pressuring her to take a drink. At first she refused – remember, she hated the taste of beer. But he was relentless and she was vulnerable. She didn't want to appear too straight-laced in front of her friends. She was more afraid of what her peers would think of her than in doing the right thing. He offered, she accepted and, as they say, the rest is history. The following are her words

> *"I took one drink and then another. Before I knew it I was pretty drunk and in one of the back bedrooms in the house with a guy all over me, taking off my clothes and having sex with me. I was willing, but unwilling at the same time. I had no control. I couldn't get him off of me, I didn't want him off of me, but I did want him off of me. It was over as fast as it began. Like a blur. And then the guilt began to sink in."*

The reason I know all of the gory details of this event is that I had come to know Sarah as a friend. As a local pastor, I would often substitute teach in the local schools to get to know the students in the community. It was a great job and it provided wonderful ministry opportunities.

Sarah did not attend the church I pastored, but we had become acquainted at school. As I said earlier, she was smart and quick-witted. We would talk about serious subjects, the future, and the plans she had for a better life, that is, until "the party."

It was a couple of weeks after "the party" when the call came. She was sobbing uncontrollably. With words that I could barely understand, she asked if I would meet her in the parking lot of the high school. It was Saturday. Like the women of John 4 who did not want to be seen at Jacob's watering well, Sarah didn't want to be seen by her friends. I agreed and made my way there realizing something was terribly wrong.

"I've missed my period and I'm pregnant!"

When I arrived she unloaded on me the story of the whole night and she then used the big "P" word – the words came out of her mouth painfully and shamefully, accompanied by many tears – "I've missed my period and I'm pregnant."

In that moment I realized that Sarah's plans for a better life had just had been put on hold. She believed her life was over. The peer pressure at "the party" and her own uncontrolled desires had produced an unwanted pregnancy and the devastation of big dreams and goals.

In that moment I realized that Sarah's plans for a better life had just had been put on hold. She believed her life was over. The peer pressure at "the party" and her own uncontrolled desires had produced an unwanted pregnancy and the devastation of big dreams and goals.

Thinking It Through

I have often thought through that entire event in my own mind. What would have happened if Sarah had maintained her otherwise confident and independent attitude and graciously declined the invitation to "the party", especially since she knew what it would be like?

What would have happened if she would have resisted one more time the temptation to take that first drink instead of wilting under the pressure of her peer? What would have happened if she had decided to leave the party once she realized things were getting out of hand? What would have happened if Sarah had planted in her mind a Scripture passage like 1 Corinthians 10:13?:

> **"No temptation has overtaken you that is not common to man. God is faithful, and he will not let you be tempted beyond your ability, but with the temptation he will also provide the way of escape, that you may be able to endure it."**

There is no excuse for the violator's behavior. And the irresponsible parents must claim a great deal of the blame for creating the conditions for such activities. There was plenty of blame to go around on this one.

But when you put yourself in vulnerable situations all too often unexpected things happen, most of which are not positive or planned.

Mom is Upset and Heartbroken!

I wish this is where the story ended for me, but it isn't. As we stood in the school parking lot, Sarah pouring her heart out to me through sobs and me listening heartbroken to her sordid story, she looked up at me and, "Will you go with me to tell my mom and dad?"

Now, I didn't know her mother or her dad, but I decided that I would not abandon her at such a critical time. What was so ironic about this was that Sarah's friends were good for a party, a drink, and some quick sex, but no one was to be found in that parking lot but a weeping, heartbroken girl, and a small-church pastor searching for words to console and comfort. It kind of made me mad at all the "players" in this scenario.

What was so ironic about this was that Sarah's friends were good for a party, a drink, and some quick sex, but no one was to be found in that parking lot but a weeping, heartbroken girl, and a small-church pastor searching for words to console and comfort. It kind of made me mad at all the "players" in this scenario.

Scared to death, I told her I would go with her. Throughout this entire process something was happening to Sarah's physical look. Sarah was a tall, slender, pretty girl with flowing brown hair and a confident walk and demeanor. But after "the party" she seemed shorter, more sullen, with eyes sunken encircled with black lines. You know what I mean. The dark natural circles around the eyes that come from stress; the dark makeup that comes from lack of sleep, worry, and anxiety. Maybelline doesn't produce this kind of eye shadow – only a sickened heart does.

Her face did not shine anymore, her walk was feeble, and her smile had all but disappeared. She was physically unrecognizable. As we drove out to her home she literally curled up in a ball in the seat next to me and sobbed the whole way home.

Once we arrived at her home, I was unprepared for what happened next. We both got out of the car and began making our way to the front door of her home. Sarah was literally up under my armpit, cowering in fear in anticipation of the response of her parents. Her mother met us at the door. I identified myself and told her we needed to talk.

As we entered the front room of that small house Sarah's mother sat on one side of the room and I sat opposite of her, with Sarah still under my arm, clinging as if to never let go. In fact, she was so close to my side, holding my arm, tears still streaming down her face, I almost sat on top of Sarah when we took our seat on the couch.

How do you deliver bad news?

Can I just say at this point that there's no good way to tell someone bad news. I have been a pastor for 28 years and I have had to deliver bad news many times. News of death, cancer, accidents, and various mishaps bring an awkwardness that is stifling. I have found it helpful to simply say it with clear and compassionate words.

I looked at Sarah's mother and said these words as if I had peanut butter stuck to the roof of my mouth, "Sarah wanted me to come with her to tell you that she just found out she is pregnant." I explained a few of the details about the events of "the party", but figured I would leave a fuller explanation to Sarah.

Rachel or Sarah Weeping?

The reaction was immediate. Sarah's mother began to weep uncontrollably. After a few minutes she gave two reasons for her grief. The first was expected. She was weeping for her daughter and the loss of her dreams. She was both angry and heartbroken.

In that moment I was reminded of Matthew 2:18 where the Bible states that when King Herod decided to kill all the baby boys two years old and younger in Bethlehem in order to destroy Jesus that "**Rachel was weeping for her children; she refused to be comforted because they are no more**." Just like those mothers who must have been inconsolable in losing their sons because of Herod's wickedness, Sarah's mother would not be comforted.

Can you imagine the grief Herod caused in Bethlehem the night of the slaughter? There is a grief that cannot be comforted, but only lived with. Sarah's mother was almost inconsolable. In that moment I fought the temptation to say something stupid as is so often the case of many people who think that flowery words can take away the pain of hurt and disappointment.

Sarah's mother's second reaction was totally unexpected. After a moment of silence, she looked up at me and told me that the reason she was weeping was that this is what had happened to her twenty years ago. Sarah had been her unexpected child. She, too, had been an "A" student with big plans to shake off the dust of this sleepy little town, go to college, and accomplish something meaningful and important.

But she had made the same mistake that Sarah had made and ended up settling into a life of mediocrity. In other words, her tears were not only for her daughter, but also for herself as she relived her own dream-killing, fear-based decisions.

Was there another way?

Think about that critical moment at "the party". A temptation was placed in front of Sarah and for fear of what her peers would think she was pressured into making a decision that would change her life forever. The fear of her peers, of what they would think or say about her drove her to make a choice that would crush her dreams and destroy her plans.

What would have happened if Sarah's fear of God had overwhelmed her fear of her friends? What would have happened if she would have fearlessly stood her ground and bravely resisted the temptation placed before her because she feared God more than she feared not being accepted by her friends?

What would have happened if Sarah's fear of God had overwhelmed her fear of her friends? What would have happened if she would have fearlessly stood her ground and bravely resisted the temptation placed before her because she feared God more than she feared not being accepted by her friends?

The desire to be accepted, liked, and appreciated by your friends is normal. But if this is what you live for – the acceptance of your friends – then the fear of not being accepted will cause you to make bad decisions that have damaging, devastating, and disastrous consequences. Galatians 6:7 is so true, **"Do not be deceived: God is not mocked, for whatever one sows, that will he also reap."**

God has woven this principle of sowing and reaping into the very fabric of human existence. It works both positively and negatively. If you sow to fear, sin, and your passionate whims you will reap what you sow. But if you sow to what is good, right, and true then you will reap the same. Sarah sowed some devastating seeds the night of the "the party" that were cultivated by fear. And the results were not pretty.

Think about it

The fears that caused Sarah to give in to the temptations that ended up short-circuiting her life were the result of the perceived threat she felt of being insulated and isolated from her friends if she did not relent, take the drink, and give herself to some stranger.

As a result, barriers were set up between her and her future, boundaries were set for her that would keep her talents under wraps, a bondage set in that stifled her freedom, and unnecessary baggage was added to her daily life. What creativity Sarah possessed was now put on hold. All because of that one moment in time when a decision was put before her and she chose out of fear.

Chapter in Review
Questions for Discussion

- Reflect on Sarah's story. Do you know anyone in your school or family with a similar story?

- How did fear play a role in Sarah's mistake?

- Have you ever been in a situation where fear caused you to make a bad decision?

- What do you make of the response of Sarah's mother, especially why she cried?

- Does this mean that fears experienced in the past never really leave us?

Chapter 13

Sarah's Story Remixed

asking and answering the 'what if' questions

Sarah's story is sad but not unusual. Is there an alternative to acting out of fear? If so, what does this look like in reality? And how can you experience making decisions that are not based upon fear, but on truth, godliness, and biblical principles? Let's place Sarah's experience under the microscope of God's Word.

The Alternative to Fear

Is there is an alternative to decisions based upon fear and peer pressure? Yes! You may not be familiar with the story of the four Hebrew boys of the Old Testament book of Daniel – Shadrach, Meshach and Abednego, along with Daniel, but it's worth a read. All four were Israelites in Babylonian captivity. That means they were a long way from home in a foreign land with lots of foreign gods and lots of pressure to conform.

In fact, Daniel 1:1-7 tells us that the king of Babylon wanted them to eat, drink, and dress in ways that were direct violations of what they had been taught from God's law. Further, the king signed an edict that every person in his kingdom had to worship Babylonian gods – symbolized in a great idol dedicated to the king himself.

And what did Shadrach, Meshach and Abednego do? They kept right on praying and serving God. God blessed all four of them with great wisdom and favor (Daniel 2:46-49). So successful were these four young men of God that jealousy among the Babylonian leaders arose.

These small-minded leaders manipulated King Nebuchadnezzar into signing a decree (Daniel 3) that said that any person unwilling to bow down and pray to their false gods would be **"cast into a burning fiery furnace."**

Soon after this decree was signed the time came for all the people to bow down and worship the golden image. What pressure! Imagine that! In the middle of the day the entire nation was required to stop what they were doing, bow down, and worship this golden image.

Again, what did Shadrach, Meshach and Abednego do? Did they melt under the fear and threat of being executed in a fiery furnace? Did they bend to the pressure? No! Instead, they refused to bow down and worship the golden image. The re-

87

sponse against them was fast and immediate (Dan. 3:12): **"There are certain Jews whom you have appointed over the affairs of the province of Babylon: Shadrach, Meshach, and Abednego. These men, O king, pay no attention to you; they do not serve your gods or worship the golden image that you have set up."** These jealous tattle tells couldn't wait to see these sons of God destroyed.

The response of Shadrach, Meshach and Abednego was equal to the accusation. Daniel 3:16-18 records their response: **"Shadrach, Meshach, and Abednego answered and said to the king, 'O Nebuchadnezzar, we have no need to answer you in this matter. If this be so, our God whom we serve is able to deliver us from the burning fiery furnace, and He will deliver us out of your hand, O king. But if not, be it known to you, O king, that we will not serve your gods or worship the golden image that you have set up."**

What an incredible answer – our God will deliver us; but even if He doesn't we will not serve false gods. These young men made a difficult decision in a moment of crisis that caused them to be delivered through a fiery trial.

The key to bravery – deciding before you have to decide

And what was the key to their fearlessness? How were they so brave? What was the source of their resolve when the moment of temptation arrived? The answer is recorded in Daniel 1:8: **"But Daniel (and Shadrach, Meshach, Abednego) resolved that he would not defile himself..."**

In other words, these four young men decided to fear God and to honor Him alone prior to the test of that commitment. This type of resolution became the foundation for resisting the temptation to give into the challenges to their faith and confidence in God. Their fear and faith in God outweighed any fear they may have experienced as a result of not being accepted or of being a part of the status quo.

In other words, these four young men decided to fear God and to honor Him alone prior to the test of that commitment. This type of resolution became the foundation for resisting the temptation to give into the challenges to their faith and confidence in God. Their fear and faith in God outweighed any fear they may have experienced as a result of not being accepted or of being a part of the status quo.

This is something Sarah had not done. How do I know this? Sarah was not a Christian. She was smart, confident in herself, and pretty. But smart, confident, and pretty are not enough to kill fear.

Only the fear killer – God – can kill the fear that you will experience when you are threatened or tempted. Christians do make mistakes. But when Christians make decisions based upon a bold faith and trust in God rather than in succumbing to the fears produced by peer pressure, they are able to avoid many of the pitfalls that come from making choices based upon fear.

Resolving to resist

Shadrach, Meshach and Abednego made some important decisions before they were tempted. They resolved to serve God. They resolved to not let themselves be violated or contaminated by worldly attitudes. And they resolved to fear God more than anything else – even more than the fear of not being accepted, the fear of paying a price for their decisions, and the fear of being different.

Chapter in Review
Questions for Discussion

- If you could have offered advice to Sarah prior to going to the party, what would you have said to her?

- Have you ever been in a situation similar to this?

- What did you do that was similar to what Sarah did? How did that decision affect your life?

- What did you do what was different than what Sarah did?

- It's easy to give advice when the pressure is not on. How do you deal with the fear of being rejected by friends or the fear that comes from peer pressure?

- What principles do you see in the lives of Shadrach, Meshach and Abednego that could have helped Sarah avoid trouble?

ONLY WHEN WE ARE NO LONGER AFRAID, DO WE
BEGIN TO LIVE.

THE FUTURE DOESN'T BELONG TO THE FAINT-
HEARTED; IT BELONGS TO THE BRAVE.

FEAR IS THE RESULT OF A POWERLESS GOD.

TRANSFORMATION

Chapter 14

The Batman Complex

It's time for the transformation from fear to fearless. The question remains, "If fear is the thing that can make you do and think crazy things, is it possible to be transformed from a fearful person into a brave individual?" Yes, it is possible. Maybe Batman can help us.

Batman Begins

The much anticipated release of the movie, *Batman: The Dark Knight*, starring Christian Bale, Michael Cain, and the late Heath Ledger did not disappoint. Not only did it set records for the opening weekend of a blockbuster movie (and a sequel at that), but gross receipts worldwide for a superhero movie eclipsed all previous box office records.

Along with *Batman Begins*, the popularity of *The Dark Knight* was due to the fact that the movie version of Batman reconnected the character to his dark, conflicted, and disturbing comic book roots. Unlike the previous Batman movies that were more "cartoonish" in nature, *Batman Begins* and *The Dark Knight* recaptured the core of Batman as an unsettled and conflicted superhero.

Batman the Beloved

But why is Batman among the most beloved of the superheroes? Unlike most other superheroes who possess some supernatural abilities, Batman (a.k.a., Bruce Wayne) is a normal guy (although he is ridiculously rich) with a superior intellect and cool tools. He's rather normal, yet abnormal.

He is driven by a mixture of the fear and loathing he experienced in the untimely and cruel death of his parents when he was a child and a dreaded and deep-seated fear of bats, both of which have been refocused into a persona that is powerful, smart, vindictive, and just outside the normal process of justice. Batman is the ultimate vigilante. In essence, Batman is a smart guy energized by fear and anger.

Batman's nemesis in *The Dark Knight* is the Joker, played by the late Heath Ledger, who himself was a conflicted person in real life. Ledger's portrayal of the Joker was so sinister, haunting, and eerie that many have predicted that Ledger's version of the Joker may go down as one of the greatest cinematic performances of a criminal, paralleling Anthony Hopkins' Hannibal Lector.

Batman and the Joker are Alike?

What is so ironic is how similar the Joker and Batman are – similar in kind, different by degree, and focus. Both are driven, both experienced bitter events in their childhood, both developed an alter-ego persona as an expression of their personal angst, and both are conflicted and disturbed.

The difference is that Batman has chosen to direct his energies toward justice, and the Joker has chosen to direct his energies toward chaos, death, and destruction. What is interesting about both Batman and the Joker is that both are driven by the element of fear.

This is not a call to take your fears and convert them into some kind of hero/anti-hero persona. It is simply a recognition of the power of fear that has been fictionalized in a comic book character. The fear Bruce Wayne experienced as a child became the driving force behind the development of his superhero persona and alter-ego.

The fear the Joker experienced as a neglected and alienated child became the driving force behind the development of an anti-hero persona. Batman directed his fears toward the dismantling of fear; the Joker directed his fears toward producing more fear and anarchy.

Real Fear is not Comical

But real fear is not fictional. Batman's struggle with fear may be fictional, but your struggles with fear are real and even more devastating. Fear can become either a curse or a blessing.

Fear can become a curse if it is allowed to boil over into a vindictive and angry attitude that disables and stops you from doing what you should do. Or, fear, properly confronted and directed, can become the force that drives you to face the challenges you encounter in everyday living.

Fear can become a curse if it is allowed to boil over into a vindictive and angry attitude that disables and stops you from doing what you should do. Or, fear, properly confronted and directed, can become the force that drives you to face the challenges you encounter in everyday living.

For example, the fearless Apostle Paul would write to Timothy, his young and often timid understudy, (2 Timothy 1:7) "**for God gave us a spirit not of fear but of power and love and self-control**." Paul wanted Timothy to avoid the cowardice that can often grip the heart (see also Romans 8:15). He would go on to urge Timothy not to let his youth become an excuse for bad behavior or a cause for indifference.

He also challenged him to "fan into flame" the gifts God had given him and to resist fear and apathy (2 Timothy 1:6). Fear will make you an apathetic coward. Fear will keep you from trying, risking, believing, and trusting. It will keep you from witnessing to the unbelieving, from challenging the status quo, from starting a Bible

study, and from taking a stand for truth and what is right.

Transforming Fear into Faith

You don't have to be afraid. What is needed is a radical transformation of your mind and heart that comes from confronting your fears and turning them into the driving force of life. The gospel is what makes this transformation possible.

Jesus Christ destroyed the power of fear by dying on a cross as a substitute for sinners shackled by sin and fear, and by being raised from the dead as the One who conquered the ultimate cause of fear – death (1 Corinthians 15).

The God who can destroy death is rightly to be feared.

In trusting Jesus Christ as Lord and Savior the fear of sin and death is dismantled and redirected toward the One who is to be feared above all things (Matthew 10:28). And when God is feared above all else He transforms us into fearless and bold disciples willing to try the new, attempt the impossible, risk for great reward, launch a new adventure, and accomplish the difficult. Look at these power verses that connect a proper fear of God with great purpose:

> **Jesus Christ destroyed the power of fear by dying on a cross as a substitute for sinners shackled by sin and fear, and by being raised from the dead as the One who conquered the ultimate cause of fear – death The God who can destroy death is rightly to be feared.**

- **"So have no fear of them, for nothing is covered that will not be revealed, or hidden that will not be known."** (Matthew 10:26)This was Jesus' encouragement to the apostles as He sent them out on mission, warning them that it would be difficult, that they would face resistance, and that they would encounter conflict. Their fear of God would become the transforming power that would conquer every challenge they faced. Fear of Him transformed them into bold believers!
- **"Therefore, knowing the fear of the Lord, we persuade others."** (2 Corinthians 5:11) Notice the connection of the ability and desire to persuade others with the gospel with the fear of God! Fearing God with a reverent respect and awe overcomes the dread you may have of witnessing to the unbelieving.
- **"Since we have these promises, beloved, let us cleanse ourselves from every defilement of body and spirit, bringing holiness to completion in the fear of God."** (2 Corinthians 7:1) You may not connect a robust fear of God with sanctification (holiness). Yet, the fear of God can drive you to be clean in body, mind and spirit. (see 1 Peter 3:15)
- **"And most of the brothers, having become confident in the Lord by my imprisonment, are much more bold to speak the word without fear."** (Philippians 1:14) Confidence in the Lord produces boldness without fear.
- **"As for those who persist in sin, rebuke them in the presence of all, so that the rest may stand in fear."** (1 Timothy 5:20) Dealing with sin happens when you are confronted in your sin so that you stand in the fear of God.

To fear God means not to fear all other things, including death. To fear all other things is to fear the wrong things, things that paralyze rather than set free. This is the great irony of the gospel. When you fear all other things you will be paralyzed by fear. But when you fear God, you are set free to be bold and confident in Jesus Christ. This is why Hebrews 13:6 says, "**So we can confidently say, 'The Lord is my helper; I will not fear; what can man do to me?'**"

The Transformation

One of my favorite scenes from *Batman Begins* is when Bruce Wayne (Christian Bale) makes his way back to the bat-infested cave that had so terrorized him as a child. At first, he falls on his knees as the fear of the swarming bats almost paralyze him.

But in a decisive moment of transformation, he stands to his feet spiritually and emotionally embracing his fear of bats that had crippled him as a young child. Wayne's submission to and embrace of his greatest fear became the most important and transforming moment of his life.

The same is true of God. God is a greatly-to-be-feared kind of God. Having no beginning and/or end, God is holy, righteous, and powerful. He is sovereign and is in complete control of all things. He is equally a God of mercy and judgment, love and justice, grace and wrath.

To fear Him is the beginning of knowledge (Proverbs 1:7; 9:10). Yet, to fear Him, to embrace Him, to submit to Him becomes the point at which our lesser fears are consumed by a greater fear that dissolves our fears. Read that again. To fear Him above all else is to be consumed by a fear that dissolves all our fears in an act of brave faith and confident trust. To fear God is to live free!

95

The Apostle John, the writer of that strange and wonderful New Testament book known as "The Revelation of Jesus Christ", wrote about his frightening encounter with the living Christ. When John saw Jesus Christ in his heavenly vision (Revelation 1:17) his reaction was immediate: "**When I saw Him (Jesus), I fell at His feet as though dead. But He laid his right hand on me, saying, 'Fear not, I am the first and the last, and the living one. I died, and behold I am alive forevermore, and I have the keys of Death and Hades (hell).'**"

To fear or not to fear? This is the question

Did you get the twist in that text? The One John most feared is the same One that said, **"Fear not…"** How is this possible? How is it possible to fear and not fear at the same time?

If fear is the threat that you sense and experience to your being and your well-being – death being the ultimate fear – then you can say in truth that to fear the One who crushed fear is to know the truth that Jesus Christ has snatched life from the clutches of death.

Embracing God in Jesus Christ conquers fear, transforming it into a reason for faith and confidence. The result will not be a superhero vigilante, but a humble yet confident person willing to try anything for God.

Chapter in Review
Questions for Discussion

- What or whom do you fear the most?

- How does that fear affect you?

- What would happen if that fear could be transformed into bravery?

- What would the fearlessness produced by such a transformation cause you to do that you're not doing now?

Chapter 15

The Fear Killer

Let me repeat, fear is the one thing that will keep you from becoming all that God intends for you to become. Fear is the great bondage-maker, keeping you from the thoughts and behaviors that lead to a life of purpose and intention. But fear is not killed the way you might think.

The main point of this book has been encapsulated in a type of logical syllogism: All people experience fear. What happens when fear is trumped by an even greater fear? And what happens when **that fear** ironically dissolves all other fears? In other words, the only way to kill fear is to rightly fear the right thing, or person, namely, God.

God Rightly Feared

When God is rightly feared a strange thing happens – your fears will dissolve into a life of courage and bravery. The transformative nature of this healthy, awe-inspired fear of God is noted in Romans 8:31, **"If God be for us, who can be against us?"** The same God who tells us to fear Him (Ecclesiastes 12:13; Matthew 10:38) also commands us not to fear anything (Isaiah 4:10; Luke 2:10; 1 John 4:18; Revelation 2:10).

If we fear (revere, defer to) God, then this kind of fear is the beginning of knowledge (Psalm 110:10), courage, and bravery (Joshua 24:14). To fear God is to have fear destroyed as you are embraced by God's all-powerful, all-loving, fear-smashing sovereign grace.

Living in a Cave?

That is why this is the most dangerous chapter you will read in this book. Let me explain. The truth that sets a per-

Becoming a fear killing person calls for a revolutionary type of shift in your thinking and feeling based upon what the fear killer has accomplished on your behalf. In other words, you no longer have to live in the cave of self-isolation and confinement. The leaflets are falling from the sky announcing a revolutionary type of freedom that allows us to live lives of ever-increasing fearlessness.

son free from fear is personal, powerful, and liberating. This is a truth that you must accept if you are to live a fearless life.

A good story illustrates this statement. In 1944 a Japanese soldier by the name of Shoichi Yokoi hid in a cave on the Island of Guam when he realized that the battle was being lost to the invading American forces. Fearing for his life, Yokoi hid in a cave and continued to live in that cave even after the battle for Gaum was over. In fact, he lived in that cave for twenty-eight years, from 1944 until 1972, coming out only at night and living off of frogs, rats, snails, shrimp, nuts, and mangoes. He made clothes for himself out of tree bark.

Read that again. He lived in a cave by himself for twenty-eight years even though he knew the war was over. He lived in fear for his life because he refused to accept the freedom that came with the ending of WWII.

When later interviewed, Yochoi said that he knew the war was over because of the leaflets that were scattered over the island jungles of Gaum, yet he was afraid that he would be executed as a military criminal. He was unaware of the terms of surrender that gave freedom and amnesty to most enemy soldiers.

Imagine the scenario. Shoichi Yokoi lived in a self-imposed, fear-induced isolation, and confinement because of fear. He was uninformed of the freedom that was his. Yochoi lived in fear because of a lie. Yochoi failed to grasp the concept that there is something even more dangerous and yet freeing than the anxiety of fear – the acceptance of the truth!

Enter the Danger Zone

The reason this chapter is so dangerous and yet so liberating is that it **1)** mentions the word God and, more importantly, the God of the Word and it **2)** calls for a Copernicus (check him out in your high school history or science book) type of revolution in your emotional and spiritual trajectory.

Before you close this chapter because of a preconceived notion of reading just another fairy-tale story about God or an "easy-believism", read on. The fear killer is not a program, although it has implications for the processes of life. The fear killer is not a new set of "how to" principles, (if I have to read one more self-help book I'm going to scream), although killing fear has practical implications. The fear killer is a person.

Before you close this chapter because of a preconceived notion of reading just another fairy-tale story about God or an "easy-believism", read on. The fear killer is not a program, although it has implications for the processes of life. The fear killer is not a new set of "how to" principles, (if I have to read one more self-help book I'm going to scream), although killing fear has practical implications. The fear killer is a person.

The Fear Killer is a Person

The argument I've been making in this book is that the fear killer is not a program or a procedure; the fear killer is a Person. Killing fear happens as a result of an ongoing relationship with Jesus Christ.

Becoming a fear killing person calls for a revolutionary type of shift in your thinking and feeling based upon what the fear killer has accomplished on your behalf. In other words, you no longer have to live in the cave of self-isolation and confinement. The leaflets are falling from the sky announcing a revolutionary type of freedom that allows you to live a life of ever-increasing fearlessness.

Since fear is so pervasive and prevalent it must be confronted and dismantled if you are to overcome the paralysis that can result from your fears. Living a life with less fear is possible only if you have your fears redirected and refocused.

Yes, you read that right. Fear is good if it is properly directed and focused. I have not been arguing for the impossible – an absolutely fear-free life. Instead, I am making the case for a properly fearful, ever-increasing life of less fear that is grounded in a confidence and courage born of a living faith in God.

Living a life with less fear is possible only if you fear the right thing. This may sound incongruent with the purpose of killing fear, but it is not. Living a fear-free life is impossible. Fear is a common feature of human existence. All people fear something. In fact, one person commented to me that people are so prone to fear that even if we do not have a fear we will make one up. The problem is that in the end you will fear the wrong things or, rather, you will fear the wrong person. An explanation is in order.

Do Not Be Afraid? Are You Kidding? NO!

If fear is the threat to your well-being and to your being itself, then fear reaches its zenith in the fear of death. All other fears are lesser forms of death. The death of a dream, of a relationship, the loss of a job, the rejection you sense from others, and the inability to attempt something great or significant are all produced by the death of courage and self-confidence. All these "lesser deaths" are but forms of the ultimate threat that produces fear – death itself.

But what would happen if the fear of death itself were removed? What would happen if the ultimate threat to your well-being and to your being itself were conquered? Would it not stand to reason that all other "lesser forms of death", all other "lesser forms of fear" would fall like dominoes under a new paradigm of thinking, feeling, choosing, and acting? Good news. Jesus Christ has conquered death. This single, but powerful truth means that living a fearless life is possible.

99

Chapter in Review
Questions for Discussion

- What do you think about the solider who lived in a cave for 28 years because of fear?

- Do you know anyone who lives like this?

- What would happen if fear were completely removed from your mindset?

- What power could be unleashed in your home, youth group, and school if fear were dismantled?

Chapter 16

A Strange Bible Passage

There is a very strange passage in the Bible regarding fear. The entire focus of Matthew 10 centers on Jesus sending out His disciples as missionaries with a message. He knew that they would face hardship and difficulties. Because of this He reminded them several times not to be afraid.

In Matthew 10:19 Jesus told His followers not be anxious. And again in Matthew 10:26 He told them not to be afraid on their mission. And then the strangest of all verses in this passage comes in Matthew 10:28, "**And do not fear those who kill the body but cannot kill the soul. Rather fear Him who can destroy both soul and body in hell.**"

What does this mean? Was Jesus sending His own disciples on some suicidal mission to prove a point? Is there a contradiction in this verse since it says not to be afraid and then to be afraid? Who kills the body but not the soul? And who is it who can kill both? Weird, huh? Read on!

Is Christianity a Fantasy?

To be quite honest, it's this kind of Bible verse that turns many people off to Christianity. Jesus' words seem like a death wish. They seem to trivialize the hardships, difficulties, and discouragements of life, especially in an age bent on self-preservation. They seem shallow and indifferent to human fear.

But are they really that shallow and indifferent? Was Jesus being insensitive? Was He so disconnected from reality that He would suggest that we should just shrug off our fears, even the fear of death?

On the contrary! Again, Jesus' words in the latter part of Matthew 10:38 are shocking, "**Rather fear Him who can destroy both soul and body in hell.**" Instead of fearing those who can only kill the body – and this would include not only other people, but cancer, sickness, wars (see 2 Corinthians 11:16-33 as an example of the sufferings of Paul) – you are to properly fear the **One** who has the ability to destroy both the body and the soul.

And who is it that has the authority and the ability to do both? Only God has the authority and the power to destroy the real you, the soul of a person. He alone is to be feared. All other fears pale in comparison to a healthy fear of God.

In the place of the disciples

Now put yourself in the place of the disciples. You have left family, friends, and the familiar to follow this nomadic teacher. If that's not enough, as He begins to define His mission in terms of sacrifice and suffering, it begins to dawn on you that there is something more rich and powerful about Jesus than His being a simple sage or a moral philosopher. And now He is sending you out on what seems like a suicide mission, as (Matthew 10:16) **"sheep in the midst of wolves."**

On top of all of this, Jesus had the audacity to tell His you not to fear because He is with you. This kind of talk is way over the top. Maybe Jesus was delusional and deceived. Unless...

We can live a fearless life only when we properly fear the only person who has the right and authority to destroy both the body (physical dimensions of life) and the soul (the real you) – God!

Fearing God as the Root of Fearlessness

Fearing God is not a popular notion. We are not supposed to fear God. In fact, to suggest that a person ought to fear God flies in the face of the kind of generic "easy-believism" that characterizes modern day spirituality.

Too often God is viewed as "the old man upstairs" or the "big guy in the sky" or the "old man in heaven who's having trouble with His spiritual, arthritic knees and He can't get down to see about us at all." Some believe that God is a great, benign teddy bear type of God who is inept and uninvolved.

This is why it will take a great deal of courage to finish reading this chapter because it will challenge some very cherished, yet erroneous beliefs about God. God is not someone we're supposed to fear. In other words, God is the cosmic teddy bear in the sky who is there to comfort the afflicted but never to afflict the comforted.

101

God has been neutered and diminished in His role as God. He has been redefined, refurbished, reinterpreted, reincarnated, and reborn in so many versions that it is often difficult to grasp a truly biblical perspective on the nature and character of God.

God has been demoted from His lofty perch as an absolutely loving, but holy God who is rightly to be feared. Yet, Scripture repeatedly makes the case that God alone is to be feared. A sample list of biblical texts reminds us of the call to fear the Lord.

- **"Now this is the commandment, the statutes and the rules that the Lord your God commanded me to teach to you, that you may do them in the land to which you are going over, to possess it, that you may fear the Lord your God, you and your son and your son's son, by keeping all his statutes and** his commandments, which I commanded you, all the days of your life, and that your days may be long." - Deuteronomy 6:1-2

- "Now therefore fear the Lord and serve him in sincerity and in faithfulness." - Joshua 24:14

- "Serve the Lord with fear, and rejoice with trembling." - Psalm 2:11

- "The fear of the Lord is the beginning of wisdom; all those who practice it have a good understanding. His praises endures forever." - Psalm 111:10
- "The fear of the Lord is instruction in wisdom, and humility comes before honor." - Proverbs 15:33

- "Since we have these promises, beloved, let us cleanse ourselves from every defilement of body and spirit, bringing holiness to completion in the fear of God." - 2 Corinthians 7:1

- "Therefore, my beloved, as you have always obeyed, so now, not only as in my presence but much more in my absence, work out your own salvation with fear and trembling, for it is God who works in you, both to will and to work for his good pleasure." - Philippians 2:12

- "Honor everyone. Love the brotherhood. Fear God. Honor the emperor." - 1 Peter 2:17

What is ironic about these texts is that they seem to contradict other Scriptures that call us to live without fear. A short list of "fear not" passages reminds us of the call to live unafraid:

- "Have I not commanded you? Be strong and courageous. Do not be frightened, and do not be dismayed, for the Lord your God is with you wherever you go." - Joshua 1:9

- "Fear not, for I am with you; be not dismayed, for I am your God; I will strengthen you, I will help you, I will uphold you with my righteous right hand." - Isaiah 41:10

- "And the angel said to them (the shepherds), 'Fear not, for behold, I bring you good news of a great joy that will be for all the people." - Luke 2:10

- "For God gave us spirit not of fear but of power and love and self-control." - 2 Timothy 1:7

- "There is no fear in love, but perfect love casts out fear. For fear has to do with punishment, and whoever fears has not been perfected in love." - 1 John 4:18

- **"Do not fear what you are about to suffer."** - Revelation 2:10

The contradiction is confusing. On the one hand Scripture tells us to fear God. Yet on the other hand, we are told not to fear. Which is it? Are you to live a life of fear or a fearless life? Maybe there is another way to look at these passages that appear, at first glance, to be contradictory. Maybe there is something else going on underneath these passages that hold them together.

Before you move forward, think again about your concept of God. If to you God is a minor character with little power, then you will always live under the weight of fear. But if there is something more to God, a power beyond all imagination, then doesn't it stand to reason that that kind of God can dismantle your fears? Doesn't it sound reasonable that you might be able to live free from fear?

Chapter in Review
Questions for Discussion

- How do you or your friends look at the claims of Christianity?

- Is the good news of Jesus Christ real? Or is it a wild fantasy?

- Why is it so dangerous to confront our fears?

- And what do you make of what appears to be contradictory statements in the Bible – we're to fear and not to fear?

- What's the difference between the two kinds of fear?

Chapter 17

Who Is In the Boat?

Let me illustrate God's command to fear and not to fear by looking at another passage of Scripture that you may have never read or even thought about.

The Transferal of Fear – Who Is This Man?
Luke 8 tells us that it had been a busy week of ministry and service for Jesus and His disciples. The disciples were frazzled with fatigue, having gone from town to town ministering to the needs of the people, preaching the good news of the kingdom of God, and learning from their master/teacher, Jesus.

For His part, Jesus was a bit weary Himself. Luke 8:19 records the efforts of His family to sidetrack Him from His ministry – they thought that He was crazy and simply needed to come home (Mark 3:31-35).

In response to His fatigue and the pressures of the crowds Luke 8:22 says that He instructed His disciples to get into a boat so that they could cross over to the other side of the Sea of Galilee. Whenever Jesus did this kind of thing, it was an indication that He had had enough of the crowds, and that it was time to be alone with His disciples and His heavenly Father.

As they crossed the sea, the next few verses of Luke 8:22-25 record one of the most amazing events in the life of Jesus and His disciples, especially when it comes to the cause and the conquering of fear. Jesus initiated this little aquatic excursion when He instructed His disciples, "**Let us go across to the other side of the lake.**"

Jesus Asleep
No sooner had they launched the boat from the shore of the Sea of Galilee then Jesus decided to take a siesta in the bow of the ship. Luke 8:23 describes Jesus' respite with simple words: "**and as they sailed He fell asleep.**" Fine companion Jesus was. He invites them to an evening on the lake only to fall asleep. Some host!

There is nothing quite wrong with the Son of Man taking a snooze as they sailed, except for what happened next. Luke 8:23 gives a description of what happened soon after their launch, "**And a windstorm came down on the lake, and they were filling with water and were in danger.**" In summary, the disciples are in the boat, a storm suddenly arises and, on top of it all, Jesus is asleep.

Storms on the Sea of Galilee were not uncommon. The Sea of Galilee is 690 feet below sea level. To the north is Mt. Hermon which rises 9,200 feet above the sea. The shape and scope of the terrain form a natural wind tunnel, especially from May to October as the warm winds sweep off the mountain top and skip across the surface of the sea causing sudden and unexpected swells and violent storms that dissipate as quickly as they form. Even though Jesus' disciples would not have been unaccustomed to such storms, the threat to their well-being and to their very being itself was nonetheless real.

They were frightened by the storm as the boat filled with water. Verse 24 describes the actions of the disciples, **"And they went and woke Him, saying, 'Master, master, we are perishing!'"** The disciples were in a panic.

Here's the scene. The disciples were about to sink in the turbulent waters of the Sea of Galilee, their fearless leader was asleep, and from all they could tell, Jesus seemed unconcerned and oblivious to the seriousness of the situation. They awakened Jesus with cries of helpless fear.

With perfect peace and serenity, Jesus did the most amazing thing – **"And He awoke and rebuked the wind and the waves, and they ceased, and there was a calm."** Did you read that? Some miracle!

Where is Your Faith?

Four things happened as a result of the disciples' distress and fear: **1)** Jesus wakes up from His slumber, which is amazing in and of itself that He could sleep in a storm. **2)** He speaks to or rebukes the wind and the waves, which give us a clue as to His divine nature. Only God can command nature in such a fashion. **3)** The storm ceases. And **4)** the most stunning calm falls over what had been a tumultuous and stormy sea. Jesus even scolds them by asking, **"Where is your faith?"**

Now you would think that this storm story would end with the disciples throwing a party and the afternoon being spent lazily basking in the sunlight of a warm day, drifting across the Sea of Galilee as Huckleberry Finn might float down the Mississippi River, skipping rocks over the glass-like surface of what was now a calmed sea. You would think that the fear of the disciples had been vanquished and conquered. Wrong!

Now you would think that this storm story would end with the disciples throwing a party and the afternoon being spent lazily basking in the sunlight of a warm day, drifting across the Sea of Galilee as Huckleberry Finn might float down the Mississippi River, skipping rocks over the glass-like surface of what was now a calmed sea. You would think that the fear of the disciples had been vanquished and conquered. Wrong! Because of what Jesus did the fear of the disciples increased.

Who's In the Boat?

Because of what Jesus did the fear of the disciples increased. Luke 8:25 records the response of the disciples, **"And they were afraid, and they marveled,**

saying to one another, 'Who is this, that He commands even winds and water, and they obey?'" *After Jesus calmed the sea, the fear of the disciples was not lessened, only transferred.* Instead of being afraid of the natural elements, they were now afraid of Him – Jesus, the One who demonstrated incredible power over the storm. They were no longer afraid of what was outside the boat because they were now afraid of what was inside the boat.

I believe this moment in the boat, and other moments like it during the earthly ministry of Jesus, became the seed of the fearlessness and boldness of the disciples that would later blossom in spreading the gospel as described in the book of Acts.

This same fear became the basis of their confidence as they faced incredible odds while spreading the gospel to a lost world. Here's just one simple description of the fear-of-God based confidence of the early disciples (Acts 9:31): "**To the church throughout all Judea and Galilee and Samaria had peace and was being built up. And walking in the fear of the Lord and in the comfort of the Holy Spirit, it multiplied.**"

Their fear of God became the basis of their fearlessness against all other fears. Ironic, is it not? Their healthy, awe-inspired fear of God outpaced and outstripped their fear of persecution, suffering, and pain. It sounds crazy, but their fear of God became the basis of their fearlessness.

Chapter in Review
Questions for Discussion

- What do you think the disciples were experiencing as the boat rocked on the sea?

- What fears were they experiencing?

- Do you think they were regretting their decision to follow Jesus Christ?

- Do you think they anticipated this kind of danger? Or do you think they expected smooth sailing, so to speak, when they decided to follow Jesus?

- What do you do when turbulent times come?

Chapter 18

How the Fear Killer Kills Fear
the death of fear and death in the death of Christ

If you can grasp the weighty truths in this chapter you will understand how fear is killed in your life.

"Death is swallowed up in victory." "O death, where is your victory? O death, where is your sting?" The sting of death is sin, and the power of sin is the law. But thanks be to God, who gives us the victory through our Lord Jesus Christ. - 1 Corinthians 15:54-57

The Death of Fear and the Death of Death in the Death of Christ

How is it possible for fear to be overcome and destroyed? How is it possible for your fear of God to become the basis of a life of fearlessness? It's actually simple, yet profound.

If fear is the threat you experience to your being and to your well-being, then what happens when that fear is dismantled? This is what God did for you in Jesus Christ. The ultimate threat to your being and to your well-being is death and God's judgment on the sin that produced death. In Jesus Christ God destroyed death. In the death and resurrection of Jesus Christ the death of death was accomplished.

The gospel is simple, yet profound. Jesus Christ, the perfect, sinless Son of God submitted Himself to the curse of death so that He might atone for your sins. He endured the wrath of God on your behalf and destroyed death from within

If fear is the threat you experience to your being and to your well-being, then what happens when that fear is dismantled? This is what God did for you in Jesus Christ. The ultimate threat to your being and to your well-being is death and God's judgment on the sin that produced death. In Jesus Christ God destroyed death. In the death and resurrection of Jesus Christ the death of death was accomplished.

107

the belly of the beast.

Jesus Christ died a substitutionary (in your place), vicarious (on your behalf), atoning (a price that was paid) death so that your sins could be forgiven, and so that the death produced by sin could be dismantled and destroyed (2 Corinthians 5:16-21). Jesus destroyed the cause of death by dying for sinners.

But this is not all. Jesus conquered the consequences of death. Jesus' resurrection from the dead overcame and destroyed death, the ultimate threat to your being and to your well-being. Again, through the resurrection of Jesus Christ, God announced the death of death and fear.

Hebrews 2:14 describes it this way, **"Since therefore the children share in flesh and blood, He Himself likewise partook of the same things, that through death He might destroy the one who has the power of death, that is, the devil, and deliver all those who through fear of death were subject to lifelong slavery."** This is absolutely stunning. Jesus took on death so that He might destroy death. And by destroying death God destroyed fear.

This is what Hebrews 2:14-15 means. Jesus took on flesh and blood, walked among us, and then died a death for us that He did not deserve so that the power of death might be destroyed in His death and through His resurrection.

As a result, if you trust in what God did in Christ you will be set free from the fear of death. You will no longer be a slave to the sin and death that threaten your very existence (Romans 6:15-23). This is why the Apostle Paul would write that in the death and resurrection of Jesus Christ, the sting of death has been removed (1 Corinthians 15:56).

The Spiritual/Copernicus Revolution

But truth unapplied is not revolutionary. What is needed is a bold and faithful commitment to the person of Jesus Christ so that a revolution, a seismic shift takes place in your heart, a radical event comparable to what Copernicus discovered. Copernicus (1473 – 1543) was that scientist who dared to suggest that the sun – and not the earth – was the center of our solar system. He was royally and religiously ridiculed because his argument altered the science of his day and challenged the authority of the church.

But truth unapplied is not revolutionary. What is needed is a bold and faithful commitment to the person of Jesus Christ so that a revolution, a seismic shift takes place in your heart, a radical event comparable to what Copernicus discovered.

Yet, he stood his ground and won the day. Now, it is hard to imagine such an antiquated concept as an earth-centered solar system. In fact, you know the universe to be much more immense than even Copernicus could have ever imagined. But the truth still remains: the daring of Copernicus' discovery altered history and changed conventional thinking. A spiritual revolution is equally disrup-

A spiritual revolution is equally disruptive. When you come face to face with Jesus Christ your self-centered ideas are ruined by His holiness. To follow Him means to make Him the center. And when He is the center the attention shifts from you to Him.

tive. When you come face to face with Jesus Christ your self-centered ideas are ruined by His holiness. To follow Him means to make Him the center. And when He is the center the attention shifts from you to Him.

You are mistaken if you believe that your fears will be destroyed by removing all minor threats; i.e. relationship risks, dangerous circumstances, challenging situations, career uncertainties, and any other issue that may threaten your life.

But this is not true. Fear is dismantled when Jesus Christ – the fear killer – enters your life, forgives your sin, heals your wounds, and gives you new life. Fear is destroyed when you are no longer the center of your own personal solar system. Jesus must become the center of your universe.

Chapter in Review
Questions for Discussion
- How does Jesus kill fear?

- What type of revolution must I experience to be different from how I am now?

- If I shifted my trust to Jesus Christ, how would my life be different?

Chapter 19

Five into Six Equals Bravery

So, how is fear worked out in your daily living? If Jesus Christ has become the source and strength of your life, how is His life in you bravely lived out? The answer is a simple, spiritual equation – five into six equals bravery. This equation does not make mathematical sense. But this chapter is not about math, it's about living a life of bravery and fearlessness. It's about being a part of something new, something fresh, bold and, life-changing.

Changing my Worldview

All of the experiences I have been talking about in this book are what may be called worldview issues. Everyone has a worldview, including you.

A worldview is how you look at things, what you think about things, and how you process information. Your worldview determines the music you like, the clothes you wear, and the ideas you believe in. Fear meets you at every point of your worldview.

If you're life is to become the radical and radiant life God desires for it to be (fearless, bold, willing, obedient) then you will need to honestly evaluate your worldview. You'll never know why you remain timid and unwilling to serve the Lord unless you do the uncomfortable work of placing every idea, feeling, and fear under the microscope of God's Word and will.

How can you begin the process of confronting your fears at the point of your worldview? Let's begin with a simple formula – five into six equals bravery. Let me explain.

Five Parts to a Worldview

Every proper worldview is made up of five parts.

God

Every worldview consists of a spiritual dimension. That is, every person asks the God questions – "Is there a god?" "If not, what does this truth mean for my life?" "If there is a God, what is God like?" "What does God want from me?" "What is God's nature?" No one, not even you, can avoid the God questions. A fully informed worldview is not complete without answering these questions. Even the atheist answers these questions – she says there is no god.

Further, if you're to make an impact on your school, home, and community you must ask and clearly answer the God questions. Your answer can be simple, but not simplistic. Your answer must be clear and concise.

Self

But the God question is not the only component of a worldview. What you think about yourself is also important. Questions like – "What and who am I?" "Am I a highly evolved animal?" "Am I a cosmic accident?" "Does life have any meaning?" Or, "Am I a special and unique creation?" "Does life have purpose that comes from outside me?" Every worldview has a category for defining the self.

If, as a Christian, you are offering people a different way of living life based upon the gospel of Jesus Christ, then they have every right to ask what that means for them personally.

You

The next question is, "What about you?" "While dealing with myself, what do I do with you?" "You're outside my body, but you're in my space." "Just who are you to me?" These are the questions of relationships. What is the nature of a meaningful relationship? How do relationships properly work? What does this mean for me and my family, for dating, for sex, for marriage, for economics, and for all kinds of relationships?

You live in a relational world. Everything hinges upon relationships. What the good news says about relationships will impact what happens in your youth group, your church, your community, and your school. People want to know how to live with themselves; they also want to know how to live in a world filled with people, most of whom are different and sometimes distant.

Vocation

Another part of a worldview is captured in the question – "What do I do with my life?" "Does my school work mean anything?" "Does writing a paper matter?" "Does my job at Dairy Queen mean anything?" This is the question of vocation. Every worldview must include the issue of work and why it matters.

The reason this is so important is because what a person does will take up most of their time. Think about. Most people use at least 40 hours of each week for school or work. If that much time is given to school and work then it is a fair question to ask – "Does work have meaning? Or, "Is my work simply something I do to get a grade or a paycheck to pay my bills?"

The gospel is able to answer this question by closing the gap between the sacred and the secular (secular here is used in a positive sense – stuff unrelated to church). In other words, does work matter to God? The answer is that work matters to God. Work is a way you can express your God-given creativity. Work is a way to glorify God (1 Corinthians 10:31, Colossians 3:17).

This is why every Christian student should strive for excellence in the classroom, the band room, in singing, and in sports. God can be glorified in the work you do.

111

Death

And what about death? Every person in every age in every culture must deal with questions like – "What happens when I die?" "When I die does I end?" "Do I simply cease to exist?" "Do I return in some cycle of reincarnation based upon what I did in life?" "Or, is there life beyond the grave?" To avoid these questions means that your worldview is incomplete.

And the gospel does answer the question of fear. Though all of us will die a physical death, those who know Jesus Christ as Lord and Savior will never die but be given eternal life (John 11).

Fear at Every Point

Fear will meet you at every point of your worldview. Fear challenges your views on God, what you think about yourself, what you think about others, how you view your work and how you view death. If Jesus Christ is the fear killer He will also meet you at every point of your worldview, answering each question and dismantling every fear at every point.

It's at these points that fear must be worked out. This happens through living a life empowered by Jesus Christ that is informed by his Word, the Bible. Bringing God's promises to bear on your fears enables you to fight the fight of faith and to overcome your fears.

> **Fear will meet you at every point of your worldview. Fear challenges your views on God, what you think about yourself, what you think about others, how you view your work and how you view death. If Jesus Christ is the fear killer He will also meet you at every point of your worldview, answering each question and dismantling every fear at every point.**

Six Promises

There are six biblical promises that can help you shape your worldview and dismantle fear through Jesus Christ.

Promise #1 – God is Sovereign

The first promise involves the character and nature of God. God is sovereign. That is, God is in charge of all things. Even when you don't understand God's ways, you can trust that God is in control.

Because God is in control, you can have confidence that God will accomplish His purposes (Psalm 47). You can also live in the confidence that nothing is out of His control or out of His sight. He knows all (omniscience), He is everywhere (omnipresent) and He is all-powerful (omnipotent).

In fact, has it ever occurred to you that nothing has ever occurred to God? God doesn't wake up each morning surprised by what happened yesterday, wringing His hands over what

> **Has it ever occurred to you that nothing has ever occurred to God? God doesn't wake up each morning surprised by what happened yesterday, wringing His hands over what to do next. He is in full control.**

to do next. He is in full control. Just ask Job (see the Old Testament book of Job). Nothing happened to Job that did not first pass through the sovereign and mighty hands of God. The same is true for you.

So, when the fear of being out of control comes your way, you can rest in the fact that God is never out of control. Nothing is ever out of His control (Acts 17:22-34).

Promise #2 – God has Spoken

Your great, sovereign God is not silent. He has spoken. God has spoken through the living Word (John 1:1), His Son, Jesus Christ (Hebrews 1:1-4) and He continues to speak through His written Word, the Bible (2 Timothy 3:16-17). The Word of God is 1) inspired, 2) authoritative and 3) useful for every area of life (2 Peter 1:16-21).

When fear threatens you, it is time to dig deep into God's Word. This is why shallow spirituality doesn't cut it. Trivial, topical, and surface oriented Bible studies will not do. Bringing to bear the promises of God on the things you fear is essential.

The power of God's Word comes from the fact that it is living and sharp (Hebrews 4:12). God's Word is also sweet, powerful, and protective (Psalm 19:7-11). To know God's Word is to know God. To know God is to know the fear killer. And to know the fear killer is to live a life set free from fear.

Promise #3 – God is our Salvation

God is also your salvation. That is, in Jesus Christ you have been set free from sin and death. If all have sinned (Romans 3:23) and the consequences of sin is death (Romans 6:23), then in Jesus Christ, sin and the power of sin have been destroyed.

God saves you by His grace as you place your faith and trust in Jesus Christ (Ephesians 2:8-10). He saves you by His mercy as well. Grace is the undeserved, free gift of forgiveness and life in Jesus Christ. Grace is receiving something you do not deserve.

Mercy is the opposite side of the coin. Mercy is the withholding of what you do deserve. So, grace gives you what you do not deserve – forgiveness, love, eternal life – and mercy keeps from you what you do deserve – wrath, judgment, condemnation (Romans 9:15; Ephesians 2:4).

113

Promise #4 – God is our Supply

One of the core roots of fear is that if you try something bold for Jesus Christ you will be left "high and dry", without any resources or strength. In Jesus Christ, God becomes your supply. Philippians 4:19-20 makes crystal clear the truth that God is your supply – "**And my God will supply every need of yours according to His riches in glory in Christ Jesus. To our God and Father be glory forever and ever. Amen.**"

When you need courage, God will supply it. When you need boldness, God will supply it. When you need wisdom, God will supply it. When you need confidence, God will supply. The God who saves you will also supply your every need

– not your every want, but your every need (Psalm 23; 2 Corinthians 9:8).

Promise #5 – God is our Sustainer

When the weight of fear is heavy on you, God will enable you to stand up under the challenges you face. The Apostle Paul found this out the hard way. According to 2 Corinthians 12, Paul was given some incredible visions of God and of heaven, so incredible that it could have made Paul arrogant and full of pride.

And what did God do in Paul to keep him from becoming too prideful? Verse 7 clearly states what God did: **"So to keep me from being too elated by the surpassing greatness of the revelations, a thorn was given me in the flesh, a messenger of Satan to harass me, to keep me from being too elated."** Scholars are unsure as to what this "thorn" was. We do know that it was a constant companion of Paul for the rest of his life.

Paul did what any person would do. He prayed and asked God to remove the thorn (vs. 8): **"Three times I pleaded with the Lord about this, that it should leave me."** God's answer to Paul must have been troubling to him at first.

2 Corinthians 12:9 is an amazing verse **"But He said to me, 'My grace is sufficient for you, for my power is made perfect in weakness.'"** Every time Paul prayed for relief, God gave him the same answer. Paul's relief was not the absence of the "thorn". Paul's relief and strength was the presence of God Himself.

> Every time Paul prayed for relief, God gave him the same answer. Paul's relief was not the absence of the "thorn". Paul's relief and strength was the presence of God Himself.

Incredible! The trouble God allowed into Paul's life became the opportunity for God to put on display His sustaining power. It's good to remember that you are not only saved by grace, you are sustained by grace even when it means that some things may never change in your life.

This is why verse 11-12 finishes the thought of God's sustaining power when Paul wrote, **"Therefore I will boast all the more gladly of my weaknesses, so that the power of Christ may rest upon me. For the sake of Christ, then, I am content with weaknesses, insults, hardships, persecutions, and calamities. For when I am weak, then I am strong."**

Think of this verse this way. Living a fearless life does not mean a life absent of hardship or challenges. It may mean a life filled with hardships and challenges that are faced with brave confidence. How is this possible? It is possible because God is the sustainer of His people, including you (Ephesians 6:10-11; Jude 23-24).

Promise #6 – God is Our Sanctification

There is one final promise. It is a promise that is described with an old, but important word – sanctification. Sanctification is the process of being set apart for a purpose. In other words, when God saves you, He begins a process in you, setting you

> The God who saves you is at work in you completing a work that will one day be finished. This is important because when fear comes your way it will make every attempt to destroy who you are and your progress in the faith.

FIVE INTO SIX EQUALS BRAVERY

apart for a great purpose. Look at this promise through the eyes of Scripture:

- **"He is the source of your life in Christ Jesus, whom God made our wisdom and our righteousness and sanctification and redemption."** (1 Corinthians 1:30)
- **"For just as you once presented your members as slaves to impurity and lawlessness, so now present your members as slaves to righteousness leading to sanctification."** (Romans 6:19)
- **"For this is the will of God, your sanctification."** (1 Thessalonians 4:3)

The God who saves you is at work in you completing a work that will one day be finished. This is important because when fear comes your way it will make every attempt to destroy who you are and your progress in the faith.

Yet, when you are in Jesus Christ, fear can be conquered because you know that God will finish His work in you because of the saving work He has already done in you through Jesus Christ. Philippians 1:6 summarizes this promise, **"And I am sure of this, that He who began a good work in you will bring it to completion at the day of Jesus Christ."**

Shaping My Worldview with God's Promises

Coming to the point of meeting the fear killer – Jesus Christ – enables us to live a fearless and bold life. By his sovereign grace he has saved us, he speaks to us through his Word, he supplies every need, sustains us when times are hard and sanctifies us so that we will one day be complete and mature.

Knowing these truths informs my worldview. For the person who has met the fear killer the God question as been answered once and for all – God is a holy and righteous God who grants grace and mercy to the repentant heart. God is sovereign and just. He will accomplish his purposes. He is in control.

The question of who I am is answered in the person of Jesus Christ, as well. Created in a the image of God for a special purpose, you are not an animal but a person with great potential and purpose that is unleashed in and through the person of Jesus Christ.

Even the question of death is given its final answer in Jesus Christ because Jesus conquered death in His death. Death died in the death and resurrection of Jesus Christ. So, if you know who God is in Christ; if you know who you are in Christ; if you know who you are as a unique creation of God; if your work can have meaning in Jesus Christ; and, if you know that death has been conquered in Jesus Christ, what is there to fear?

The question of who you are to me has been answered in Jesus Christ, as well. Just like me, you are a unique creation of God who can engage in meaningful relationships.

The question of what I do with my life is answered in God's promises because he has called each of us to a life of purpose that glorifies him. This means that whether or not you work at Pizza Hut or envision yourself as a future CEO your work can have meaning if it glorifies God and ministers to others.

Even the question of death is given its final answer in Jesus Christ because Jesus conquered death in his death. Death died in the death and resurrection of Jesus Christ. So, if we know who God is in Christ; if I know who I am in Christ; if I know who you are as a unique creation of God; if my work can have meaning in Jesus Christ; and, if I know that death has been conquered in Jesus Christ what is there to fear?

This sounds simple, but it's really true. Conquering fear is a one-time event when Jesus Christ encounters our lives. But it is also a daily battle as we shape our worldview according to the promises of God.

Putting it Together

In summary, how can you get your mind around the equation, five into six equals bravery? How is it possible to evaluate and alter, if necessary, your worldview based upon the promises of God? Here's a possible way to think through this equation.

Your belief in God reminds you that He is sovereign and in control so that even when you don't understand every event in life you can trust Him. It also tells you that He is loving, gracious and, merciful. He is holy, righteous (sinless), and perfect. Further, God is concerned about His creation, including you.

This will lead you to the second question. The truth about God gives you a clue as to who you are. As a unique creation of God, you are not an animal, nor an accident. You have meaning. You have purpose. There is significance to your life. It also means that things are not as random and as out of control as they appear. As a result, your identity is found in your Creator and not totally in you. The One who made you has the right to define you. As a creation of God you have worth.

As a unique creation of God you can have meaningful relationships with others. Instead of arrogance and insecurity dictating how you relate to others, your identity in Jesus Christ releases you to relate to others with grace, love, and understanding.

And what about that job you have? Because God exists and has defined who you are, your school work, your writing, your interests, and your creative expressions become opportunities for self-fulfillment and for glorifying God.

And when death comes you will be ready because the One who has conquered death lives in you.

116

Chapter in Review
Questions for Discussion

- What are the five parts of a worldview?

- How do they work?

- What do I think about each of the parts of my worldview?

- What promises can you count on to battle fear?

- How do the promises of God shape your worldview?

Chapter 20

You Can't Live Where You Visit
leaving the mountain to the live in the valley of fears

We have come to the end of the journey of conquering fear. I have made every attempt to talk about every aspect of fear. And I have made every effort to explain the liberating, life-changing, fear-killing nature of the person of Jesus Christ. Knowing Him kills fear.

But the truth of the fear-killing power of Jesus Christ will remain words on a page unless you put your full confidence and faith in Jesus Christ. You cannot afford to be an "empty suit."

It's time to set aside this book and face real fear, real life. It's time to go to school and face your friends and enemies. It's time to head back home where things are tense and uncomfortable. It's time to witness to that friend that you have been avoiding. It's time to start that Bible study that you think no one will attend. It's time to try, to risk, and do great things for God. It's time to put yourself out there in harms way. It's time to leave the mountain of experiencing life in Jesus Christ to see if it works in real life. I promise – it does.

The Temptation to Not Change

The temptation will be for you to play it safe, to hide yourself in your youth group or among your small group of friends. The temptation will be for you to continue to live in fear.

> The temptation will be for you to play it safe, to hide yourself in your youth group or among your small group of friends. The temptation will be for you to continue to live in fear.

You cannot be like the disciples in Matthew 17:1-13. They had followed Jesus to the top of a mountain outside the city of Jerusalem. It was there that Peter, James, and John saw Jesus "transfigured" (glorified) before their very eyes. In fact, the Bible tells us that Moses and Elijah visited with Jesus. It must have been one incredible sight.

This event blew the minds of Peter, James, and John. Peter, always the first to speak, expressed the feelings of the other two when he said (Matthew 17:4), "Lord, it is good that we are here. If you wish, I will make three tents here, one for you and one for Moses and one for Elijah." In other words, Peter had had such a phenomenal worship experience seeing Jesus glorified with the glory He had before coming to earth that he (James and John, too) wanted to stay on the mountain with Jesus, basking in the glow of His glory.

Jesus would have none of it. Matthew 17:7 gives this stunning description of how Jesus responded to Peter's offer: "**But Jesus came and touched them, saying, 'Rise, and have no fear.'**" I love that last phrase, "...have no fear." Jesus' command was not a denial of the need for worship. In fact, what they had seen had wonderfully frightened them. This event would become one of the seeds that would eventually blossom into fearlessness.

What happened next is amazing as well. They descended the mountain and witnessed Jesus healing a demon-possessed boy (Matthew 17:14-21). Jesus was teaching His disciples a lesson about life and fear. While it may be safe to stay on the mountain, it's not where life is lived.

This is true for you as well. If you have met Jesus Christ, if you have seen His glory in His grace, in His holiness, and in His sovereignty then you cannot play it safe. Fear is gone. Boldness has come. It's time to live it out.

Leaving the Mountain

In 1994 my family and I visited my parents in Anchorage, Alaska. The visit was incredible. God did "real good" when He made Alaska.

During our visit we decided to go camping for a couple of days at the base of Mt. McKinley (Denali). Denali, the Alaskan Indian name for the highest mountain in North America (20,000 plus feet tall), means "the big one", the "high one". Denali is so tall that it makes its own weather.

We also found out a very interesting fact about Denali. Approximately 10,000 people attempt to climb it every year, with about 8,000 actually succeeding. To hear the stories of those who succeed in climbing this mammoth mountain is thrilling.

But we also learned another thing about Denali. No one lives on the mountain. Did you get that? No one lives on the mountain. It's too high, the air is too thin, and it's too dangerous. It's great to visit its peaks, but you simply can't live in its rarified air or survive its tumultuous storms.

Even though you can't live on the mountain, those who climb its peaks say that the mountain lives in them. It is said that once you visit the top of Denali you will carry that experience with you for the rest of your life. It's OK to visit its heights, but you just can't live there.

This is the challenge before you. Attending an awesome week-long camp or sensing the presence of God in a worship service at your church is great. But this is not where life is lived. As a Chris-

This is the challenge before you. Attending an awesome week-long camp or sensing the presence of God in a worship service at your church is great. But this is not where life is lived. As a Christian, you can no longer hide yourself in your church or in your small protected youth group. It is time for you to climb the mountain of God and to look into the face of God and be awed and stunned by the beauty of His presence and the power of who He is (Exodus 33:7-23).

tian, you can no longer hide yourself in your church or in your small protected youth group. It is time for you to climb the mountain of God and to look into the face of God and be awed and stunned by the beauty of His presence and the power of who He is (Exodus 33:7-23).

But once you've experienced Him you must descend the mountain and go live in the valley with your friends and family members, fearlessly and boldly telling them that the climb was worth it, challenging them to make the climb for themselves.

So, God is moving. Will you respond? Will you leave the next youth conference, the next camp meeting, or the next worship service at your church only to chicken out when it comes to telling the story of the awesome God you serve? Or, will you leave the mountain with the mountain in you to live without fear?

Kevin Shrum lives like you. He has been a teenager, is a husband, dad, and pastor. Teens hang out in his house all the time. He cares about you and how fear has affected your life. His publisher is making him tell you he is a Dr. and has a Divinity degree and serves as the pastor of Inglewood Baptist Church. Kevin doesn't really care about all of that.

John Pisciotta is the creative guy for Ripcord Entertainment. He's an award winning record producer and business owner who has helped hundreds of artists, bands, writers, and friends to use their gifts fearlessly. He loves to multiply talent.

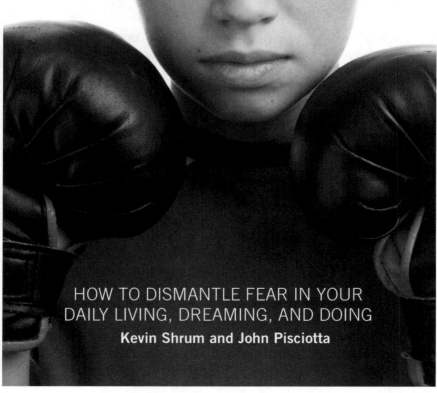